D1272943

Ships' Figureheads

Ships'

1469 Morstein Road, West Chester, Pennsylvania 19380

Foreword

"Neptune's wooden angels", as figureheads have been called, have been able to draw the visitors of nautical collections under their spell more strongly than many other objects. Usually they are the last remaining parts of hundreds of ships that have not themselves survived. The very fact that figureheads have been preserved when an old ship was scrapped or a ship's wreckage was washed up on the shore shows the high esteem they have enjoyed. Figureheads embodied the individuality of a ship, not only for their crews, but also for the rest of the coastal population. The present-day observer, who is not as familiar with old sailing ships as the people who lived with, on and from them, will not have an easy time finding in the figurehead the soul it expressed of the ship it adorned. The figures themselves tell very little of the measurements and designs of the ships of the past. When a figurehead was found on the shore, the name of the ship was often not known. Archaeologists do not usually find the figures from earlier eras along with the entire ship, but as loose fragments. Difficult "translation" work must be done before one can form a concrete conception of the whole ship.

At the same time, their display in temperature-controlled museum rooms requires the greatest possible dissociation that one can impose on this art that has been torn away from its original surroundings. Figures of saints, for instance, that have been taken from an altar and thus withdrawn from the liturgical context for which they were created, were at least intended for an enclosed area, which the museum room offers them. Figureheads on the other hand are exterior works of art that neither stood alone in parks nor decorated the vertical walls of buildings, so they look quite remarkable on the walls of museum rooms. They were the specific decoration for the complex forms of naval architecture, and can only be understood in their specific inclinations when one knows the bow design to which they were added. But even when they are displayed at the original angle, in the museum they lack not only their relationship to the ship's hull for which they were created, but also, and especially, their relationship to the endless horizon of the sea at which they cast their eyes.

Probably it is exactly this look into the distance that impresses the observer. For their effect depends least of all on their artistic quality, which covers a very broad spectrum from down-to-earth carving to outstanding artistry. What is decisive is the desire to give human or even animal qualities to the characteristics and tasks of the ship, from which one may get an impression of, for example, pride or friendliness, relaxed strength or threat, elegance or purposeful striving. May the reader find pleasure in rediscovering these qualities in the selections included here from the general catalog of the existing specimens of figureheads that was published in cooperation with the Deutschen Schiffahrtsmuseum, and which has since gone out of print.

Prof. Dr. Detlev Ellmers
Managing Director of
the Deutschen Schiffahrtsmuseums

The letters and numbers in parentheses in the text are the identification numbers under which the objects are registered in the general catalog of the Deutschen Schiffahrtsmuseums. Here the first letters are the international motor vehicle code for the country. This is likewise true of the captions in the photo section, pages 49 to 127.

A=Austria, AUS=Australia, B=Belgium, BDS=Barbados, BG=Bulgaria, BR=Brazil, CDN= Canada, CH=Switzerland, CO=Colombia, D=Federal Republic of Germany, DDR=German Democratic Republic, DK=Denmark, E=Spain, F=France, FJI=Fiji, GB=Great Britain, GBG=Guernsey, GBJ=Jersey, GBM=Isle of Man, GBZ=Gibraltar, GR=Greece, I=Italy, IL=Israel, IS=Iceland, J=Japan, MS=Mauritius, N=Norway, NL=The Netherlands, NZ= New Zealand, P=Portugal, PL=Poland, R=Rumania, RA=Argentina, RCH=Chile, RI= Indonesia, S=Sweden, SF=Finland, SU=Soviet Union, TN=Tunisia, TR=Turkey, USA= United States of America, YU=Yugoslavia, ZA=South Africa.

Hans Jürgen Hansen

Clas Broder Hansen

Figure heads

The decorative
bow figures of ships

With a foreword
by Museum Director
Prof. Dr. Detlev Ellmers

Published in
cooperation with the
Deutschen Schiffahrtsmuseum,
Bremerhaven

Copyright © 1990 by Urbes Verlag Hans Jürgen Hansen.
Library of Congress Catalog Number: 90-63800.

All rights reserved. No part of this work may be reproduced or used in any forms or
by any means—graphic, electronic or mechanical, including photocopying or
information storage and retrieval systems—without written permission from the
copyright holder.

Printed in the United States of America.
ISBN: 0-88740-299-2

We are interested in hearing from authors with book ideas on related topics.

Published by Schiffer Publishing, Ltd.
1469 Morstein Road
West Chester, Pennsylvania 19380
Please write for a free catalog.
This book may be purchased from the publisher.
Please include $2.00 postage.
Try your bookstore first.

Introduction

Figureheads are the carved wooden figures, usually brightly painted, that decorated the bows of almost all larger ships into the last century. They have an old tradition, and there must have been hundreds of thousands of them in the course of nautical history. Those that are still in existence today have been tracked down by the Deutsche Schiffahrtmuseum in Bremerhaven, registered and published in 1979 as the appendix to my history of figureheads. This was done with the kind cooperation of nearly all the museums and collections in the world that contain figureheads, as well as numerous scholars and hobbyists whose interests include this area which is still seldom researched but constitutes a significant part of maritime and artistic history.

Because the original catalog has gone out of print, the many new readers have access only to this new edition. It includes a great many of the pictures and all the color plates, but not the catalog appendix.

The photo captions have been written by my son Clas Broder, who gathered and expertly organized a great deal of material for the original edition, particularly from the British Isles.

Almost 1800 objects from 22 countries have been catalogued by the Deutschen Schiffahrtsmuseum. But what has become of the hundreds of thousands, or even millions, of other figures that once existed? When ships were built exclusively of wood, as they were until into the 19th Century, they were dismantled when no longer seaworthy (and had not been lost in shipwrecks). Useful pieces of wood were reused for building purposes, and the rest as fuel in a day that knew neither coal nor oil. This was the fate of the figureheads too, if they were in bad condition. But well-preserved specimens were usually taken home by one of the ship's carpenters, foremen, or the ship's owner or captain. Here they usually found a place in the garden or on a gable wall, until they too rotted away and were burned.

Even at the beginning of our century, figureheads were seen all along the coasts, having come from wrecked or stranded ships or been washed ashore from sunken ships. Most of them have gone to ruin since then; relatively few passed into the hands of collectors or into the possession of local or seafaring museums at the right time, assuring their preservation.

Several significant collections were essentially assembled from such figureheads, found in gardens or on the walls of houses, such as the unique one at the Skagens Hotel an the northern tip of Denmark and broken up before World War II; the collection of Captain Long John Silver, displayed in the Cutty Sark at Greenwich; and that on the Isle of Tresco in the Scilly Isles.

Other figureheads of the past that still exist mostly came from naval fleets, where it was the custom to keep the figureheads of decommissioned or scrapped ships in arsenals, especially those from ships that took part in renowned expeditions or sea battles. But in naval depots too, figureheads were often set up outdoors and thus exposed to weathering. Some of these have also made their way into maritime museums in recent years.

According to the general catalog of the Schiffahrtsmuseums, of the nearly 1800 figureheads and other carved bow decorations that are still in existence only a total of four prehistoric and Viking-era pieces were made before the 16th Century. The earliest surviving figurehead that has been precisely dated and located, of which even the name of the sculptor who carved it is known, is the lion from the Swedish warship *Wasa*, dating from 1628. Only seven other surviving figureheads definitely originate from the 17th Century; from the first half of the 18th there are ten, and from the period between 1750 and 1880 there are about sixty. All the others were created in the 19th and 20th Centuries. When one considers that a good hundred of these were carved in the years since 1900, it means that the majority, some 90%, of those in public and private possession today come from the 19th Century.

In this era, some thousand ships ran ashore on the Scilly Isles off the southwestern tip of England, out of whose wreckage approximately fifty figureheads were salvaged and are preserved there in the old abbey of Tresco on the island of the same name. That is about 5%, which makes clear the quantity of figureheads that were lost in the world in the last century.

On the other hand, one may assume that of the sculpted works that were created on dry land in those hundred years, at least half have survived. And if one extends such comparisons into the 18th and 17th Centuries, and even to earlier centuries from which not a single figurehead remains but plenty of "landlubber" sculptures exist in churches, castles and museums, it becomes clear that the figureheads and other carved decorations of ships—for lack of material to observe—have only rarely been looked upon with favor by the art world. In not one single general work that deals with the history of sculpture have figureheads been mentioned or illustrated.

May this book, then, as we wished for the first edition, inspire interest in one of the most original and traditionally rich areas of international sculpture to the extent its cultural and artistic significance deserves.

Hans Jürgen Hansen

Sacrificial Animals and Eyes

The ancient custom of decorating the bows of ships probably had cultic origins. Southern Egyptian and Nubian rock drawings from pre-dynastic times, more than five thousand years old, show oar-powered boats with high prows crowned by the head of a horned animal. The carvings on an Egyptian bone tablet from about 2700 B.C. also show a horned animal head on the stem of a boat; and a rock drawing from the shore of Lake Onega in Russia, from the 1st Century B.C., obviously shows an oar-driven boat with a similar bow ornament. Heads of horned animals such as deer, antelopes or bulls also decorate a series of bronze ship models from Sardinia, dating from the 7th and 8th Centuries B.C. It is not definite whether all these portrayals represent carved heads or the original heads of sacrificial animals that were mounted on the prow.

The British geographer Hornell reports that on the Coromandel Coast of India about a hundred years ago, when ships were launched, sheep were sacrificed and their heads stuck on the point of the bow. And according to the same source, sheep's fleeces were nailed onto the prow when Arabian ships were launched. This custom of placing the pelt of a sacrificial animal on the stem was already customary in the Mediterranean in ancient days. Usually it was sheep, rams, or lambs that were sacrificed, and their fleeces have been represented in carved wood on the stem crowns of Italian fishing boats to this day. The Museo Storico Navale in the Venice arsenal has such a carved fleece from the prow of an Adriatic trabacle from the 19th Century.

The Greek saga of the Golden Fleece, the precious sheepskin guarded by a dragon on the shore of the Black Sea that Jason and his Argonauts stole from King Aetes with the help of the king's daughter Medea and took with them on their subsequent journeys, also refers to the ancient belief in sacrifice that goes back into the dawn of history along the Mediterranean shores and gave rise to this old tradition. Fleeces decorate the prows of fishing boats on the St. Peter's Altar, painted in 1411 by Luis Borassa, in St. Mary's Church at Tarrasa, near Barcelona. A fleece also crowns the stem of a sailing ship in a storm on a votive panel of 1608, decorated with many other votive pictures of maritime scenes, from the Madonna dell'Arco Church in Naples, that has been preserved in the Arsenal at Venice.

In these pictures, of course, it cannot be seen whether they are carved wooden representations of fleeces or real ones covering the head of the stem, or even imitation fleeces of rope, such as are found to this day on fishing boats on the Algarve Coast of Portugal.

When the finished hull of a ship was launched, an animal was sacrificed, its blood annointing the bow and its head or skin being used to adorn the prow. Since the 18th Century, champagne, bubbling from a bottle broken against the bow, has been used in place of a sacrificial animal's blood; the fleece has given way to a carved imitation, and the skull to the carving of a figure, the subsequent figurehead.

The animal's head as a decoration for the stem may have served to exorcise spirits or appease the powers of nature personified by a god; on the other hand, this head at the point of the prow may indicate that the ship itself was regarded as a living being with a head and a tail.

A fleece as a stem crown in a votive picture from the Church of Madonna dell'Arco in Naples, dating from 1608, in the Museo Storico Navale of Venice.

An even more obvious reason for equating a ship with a living creature are the eyes that have decorated both sides of the bows of ships since ancient times. It is found in many cultures and on many coasts, in Portugal, all over the Mediterranean, in India, Indonesia and China. This symbolic eye, the oculus of antiquity, that turns the ship decorated with it into a living creature, an aquatic animal, has a tradition scarcely less antique than the fleece. Probably it also goes back to pre-dynastic times in Egypt, where it later became the widespread symbol of the sun god Hurus. It is found in hieroglyphic inscriptions as well as in decorations on burial gifts. Through the extensive maritime connections of the Egyptians, this symbol spread throughout the Mediterranean and probably via the Red Sea to the Indian Ocean too. The early seafarers of the Cyclades, Crete, pre-Hellenic Greece and Phoenicia used it on their ships. As early as the 7th Century B.C. it appeared in Etruscan wall paintings in Italy, and after that it was seen on all the antique coins on which ships were depicted. Behind the beak-like bowsprit that is to be seen in most other surviving portrayals of antique Greek and Roman ships, these eyes really gave them the appearance of a fearful sea monster. Painted on the bow in bright, lively colors, they are still seen today on fishing boats and small freight vessels of the Algarve, Sicily and the Adriatic, on the coasts of Java and China. In India and Ceylon a ship painted with the eyes represents a Hindu god with whose spirit it is christened when launched. The eye appears on a ship model from Cyprus, dating from about 600 B.C., as well as on the bow of the stone carving at Neumagen on the Moselle, a work almost a thousand years newer, which portrays a Roman river ship laden with wine barrels.

10

Stem Heads

The high-rising stems of the Roman ship portrayed at Neumegen end in animal heads, both looking forward; the forward one is that of an animal resembling a dog, or perhaps a dragon, the rear one is presumably a lion. Fragments of other Roman sculptures in the form of ships also show animal heads as stem figures, such as the fragment of a marble spring in the form of a ship's bow, dating from about A.D. 30, at the Museo Nuovo Capitolino in Rome. Here the scaly upper body of a dragon is seen, with a boar-like head and a suggestion of wings. Similarly, a boar- or bear-like head decorates the stem of the *Navicello*, the marble model of a Roman warship from the time of Christ's birth, which has stood in front of the Church of Santa Maria in Domenica in Rome since 1513 (with considerable Renaissance restoration).

The long-necked wooden animal heads, made in the time of the tribal emigrations, that have been found in the sediments of the lower Schelde also seem to be stem figures. They have been dated individually by the radiocarbon method. The oldest comes from the middle of the 4th Century, was found near Moerzeke-Mariekerke, and portrays an unreal creature with a mouth like a bill; one about a hundred years newer, found near Appels, has a round head and sharp teeth. Both figures are found in the British Museum. The third, one to two hundred years newer, which was found near Zele and belongs to the Antwerpener Schiffahrtsmuseum, looks most like a snake's head. It is quite possible to regard it, and the other two, particularly on account of their long thin necks, as snake-like or dragon-like fairytale creatures that once symbolized the ships on whose stems they were mounted.

Whether the boats that once traveled on the Schelde were Frankish, Friesian, or Anglo-Saxon can no longer be determined. Perhaps they even resembled the Viking longships which landed along the Schelde, Seine, Rhein, Weser and Elbe around 800 and despoiled Europe.

The truly splendid Viking ship, richly decorated with carvings, that was found around 1900 in a burial mound near Oseberg on the west shore of the Oslo Fjord and dates from around 800, has high stems ending in spirals. The front post portrays the coiled neck and head of a snake, whose body blends into the hull of the ship and at the sternpost ends in a spiral resembling that of the bow, the end of which forms the snake's tail.

The very portrayals of Viking ships and Gotland carvings of the past century show these typical spiral-shaped bow and stern posts. Any unearthed Viking-era ships, though, share a lack of carved prow decorations. Yet spiral forged iron decorations, obviously meant to ornament the prow, have been found on the Viking-era Ladby Ship discovered in the Roskilde-Fjord in Denmark. The mold for an iron dragon's head, dating from about the same time and discovered at the Viking harbor town of Birka near Stockholm, resembles not only the ancient heads from the Schelde but also the stem posts of the ships with which William the Conqueror landed in England in 1066. They are portrayed in the great Bayeux Tapestry in the town hall of Bayeux, made just a few years later.

The tapestry shows, as does the completely preserved animal head from Appels on the Schelde, that the dragon heads of Germanic ships were removable. What they were meant to portray can be told from the Old Icelandic Vlfjot Law, according to which the Vikings—in order to bring them good luck and their enemies bad luck on their raids—set dragon heads on the prows of their ships at the beginning of their trips but removed them on the return trip before reaching home, so as not to frighten the good spirits of their lands. On the ships shown on the Bayeux Tapestry and the Moselle ship at Neumagen, the animal heads on the bow and stern are both facing forward. This was already true of the wonderfully worked antelope heads on the model Nile boat found in the grave of Tutankhamun, from about 1350 B.C. The same is true of a miniature in Harleian Manuscript 4751 in the British Museum, dating from the 12th Century, and on a seal of the Hanseatic city of Lübeck made in 1226. It happens just as often, though, that the head of the stem post looks forward, that of the stern post backward, i.e., in the relief carvings on the baptismal font in the Church of St. Lawrence in Zedelgem, West Flanders, and in Winchester Cathedral, as well as the picture of the Minnesänger Friedrich von Hausen sailing to the Holy Land in the Manesse Manuscript, made shortly after 1300. The two animal heads on the bow and stern posts of the sailing ship carrying armed warriors, seen in a wall painting dating from about 1350 in the church at Skamstrup, Denmark, also look to the front and rear respectively.

But in a number of medieval miniatures the bow and stern decorations of ships are very clearly characterized as unique living creatures, such as the ship on a page of the Speyer Evangel of 1198 in the State Library at Karlsruhe, which is ornamented with a dragon- or wolf-type animal head at the bow and a wolf's bushy tail at the rear. The bow and stern ornaments in portrayals of ships in Manuscript CCC157 at the Bodleian Library at Oxford and Manuscript 9916 at the Royal Library in Brussels, both dating from the 12th Century, are clearly differentiated as heads and tails.

The decorated stern post disappears during the course of the 13th and 14th Centuries with the introduction of the stern rudder, because its shaft probably could not be turned if it included a high post with a carved figure. Instead, carved symbolic figures are later found at the top of the rudder blade. These can be dated, though, only back to about 1600, and it is thus not definite whether they directly assumed the function of stern-post figures.

Picture at right: The bow of the Moselle ship at Neumagen, with dragon's head and oculus, a Roman grave monument dating from about A.D. 300. State Museum, Trier.

13

Dragon Heads

Most of the early and middle medieval stem figures, beginning with the strange heads from the Schelde and even those of the Roman Moselle ship, seem to portray snake- or dragonlike creatures. Their features, often portrayed in very primitive style, are either lizard-like or resemble wolves or even dogs.

In the early Middle Ages the dragon was a figure based on Oriental and antique models, and was carried on a flag by an army in battle as its symbol. To the Germans this fabulous creature in its classic form, with two clawed feet, small upraised wings, a lizard-like, sometimes bird-like or even wolf-like head, forked tongue and snake-like tail, was first met as the symbol of Roman cohorts. Perhaps the figure of this ancient mythical beast was also linked with gigantic reptilian monsters from Germanic mythology, such as the Lindwurm or the Midgard serpent.

The fact that the dragon's head on the stem of a ship had a similar military significance to that used as a symbol by the Roman cohorts in battle is shown by its appearance in almost all surviving medieval pictures of ships, for those that show stem figures, almost always in dragon form, are armed warships.

Until the end of the 16th Century, most warships from the Baltic and North Seas have a bow figure of a dragon as a frightening symbol of strength and fighting spirit. On unarmed merchant ships, on the other hand, one scarcely finds dragon heads or traces of other bow figures, neither on the one original Hanseatic cog from about 1380 which survives in the German Maritime Museum in Bremerhaven; nor on the *Knorren*, the Viking freight boats that have been discovered, which, unlike the slender longboats in which the Nordic conquerors went into battle, served peaceful purposes.

On one of the numerous panels of the great winged altar that Master Bertram created for St. Peter's Church in Hamburg in 1379 there is a scene showing the building of Noah's ark. This "ark" has the typical stern of the cog of those days, with a straight stern post carrying a high, thin rudder blade with Gothic iron fittings. The design of the tiller no longer allows any stern ornament, such as still can be seen in the wall painting at Skamstrup, a few decades older, or in a print of the city seal of Bergen dating from 1376. The head of the stem in Bertram's ark, though, is more like a dog than a dragon and yet very similar to those of the Skamstrup ship or the one on the Bergen seal.

As the rudder controls and the sterncastle that was already taking shape in the 13th Century caused the head of the stern post to disappear, the stem post was replaced with the forecastle that was found on most large ships as of 1400. Over the prow there was now a triangular forecastle, proceeding from the forward deck beams and with its point projecting far forward. Its front end was set on a beam extending far forward, the point of which, like the upward-pointing prow itself in earlier times, ended in a carved animal head.

Again, these were usually dragons' heads. Above all, they decorated the armed carracks and caravels of the Portuguese and Spanish explorers in the 15th Century. These almost horizontally extended dragon heads with all their woodwork under the forecastle are particularly clear to see in a miniature showing carracks in a Flemish

Left: A one-masted warship with a dragon's head decorating its stem; chalk painting in a church at Skamstrup, Denmark, circa 1350.

Right: The building of the ark, a panel of St. Peter's Altar by Master Bertram, painted in 1379, with an animal's head crowning the stem; Art Hall, Hamburg (the part of the ark painted over in the 17th Century is indicated by lines).

manuscript at the Viennese National Library (Cod. 2533, Fol. 109 r); on a model carrack in the Prince Henry Museum in Rotterdam, dating from about 1450 and coming from the Costa Brava port of Mataró; on the Schlüsselfeld Cup, a wine beaker of 1503 made of gilded sheet silver in the form of a carrack, at the Germanic National Museum in Nürnberg; on a similar work of Parisian goldsmithing of about the same age at the Victoria and Albert Museum in London; in a water-color by Hans Holbein the Younger in the Städel Art Institute in Frankfurt; and in a painting of the embarkation of Henry VIII at Dover in 1520, owned by the Queen of Great Britain and likewise (though probably wrongly) attributed to Holbein but probably painted around 1550.

None of the dragon heads that once decorated the foremost point of these ships has survived. Yet perhaps the dragon in an oaken sculpture of St. George carved in 1544 at Antwerp, one of the world's most important ports and shipbuilding centers at that time, may give an idea of how the originals of these threatening animal heads looked on the bows of ships.

15

Fore- and sterncastles, though, were often decorated with coats of arms, and often the bow figure, the dragon or other animal head, was lacking. Such castles studded or painted with coats of arms are seen on the ships in a scene from the life of St. Nicholas, painted by Ambrogio Lorenzetti in 1332, in the Uffizi of Florence. A city coat of arms of Kiel, of about the same age, shows the arms of Holstein on the bowsprit of a cog, and through all the 15th and most of the 16th Century, these colorful rows of emblems were found on the castles of warships, and shown perhaps most impressively in the aforementioned painting of the embarkation of Henry VIII.

At times the projecting beam ahead of the forecastle also bore the figure of a saint. The form of St. Catherine is known to have been used in this position, and a votive picture from 1489 in St. Mary's Church in Lübeck shows St. George standing with shield and banner next to the bowsprit of the ship that is shown wrecked in the picture.

Left: Dragon figure of oak, a detail of a statue of St. George, carved in 1544, at the Vleeschhuis Museum in Antwerp.

Right: Figurehead lion from the Swedish warship *Wasa*, carved by Marten Redtmer in 1628; Statens Sjohistoriska Museum, Wasavarvet, Stockholm.

Figurehead Lions

Toward the end of the 16th Century the dragon began to disappear as a figurehead. The three-masted galleons, the large sail warships that were customary now, no longer had a triangular forecastle projecting out over the prow, but instead a new type of design, the *Galion* figurehead that took its name from this type of ship, on which it made its first appearance.

The beam projecting forward over the prow from the middle of the foremost deck beam, on which the forecastle rested in the carracks, and whose upper end generally formed the dragon's head, was now more or less replaced by two beams set farther to each side of the prow and extending far forward. They carried the basket-like, pointed figurehead framework, from which the crew could handle the sail attached to the bowsprit. In battle the bowsprit served as a boarding bridge, and in everyday life at sea it was the lavatory, with the crew using the lee side.

Up front, at the tip of the lower bowsprit beam, there now stood the figurehead, usually life-sized, as the successor to the animal head formerly carved out of the stem. Taking its name from the galleon of the Renaissance, it has retained it to this day, although galleons and their *Galion* figures have disappeared from the world's oceans.

Since the end of the 16th Century, though, the medieval dragon, symbol of power and fighting spirit that had stood atop the stem post, became very uncommon. No longer was a mythical creature seen there, but rather an animal whose mythic-symbolic tradition goes back into ancient cultures just as far as the dragon. It was the lion that began to play a leading role in heraldry as well as in art and architecture toward the end of the 16th Century, as a doorway guardian and a decorative figure in other ways. It maintained this prominence throughout the entire Renaissance and Baroque eras.

In Germany the lion, under the influence of ancient days, was regarded as the king of the beasts since about the 9th Century, replacing the bear that the Germanic peoples had previously used. In individual caes the lion had already been used as a bow ornament before that. Ships with lion bow figures are shown in a rock relief in the Egyptian Valley of the kings that portrays the battle of Pelesium in 1180 B.C.

It may have been important in the transition that the House of Tudor, which held the British throne from 1485 to 1605 (with its most famous rulers Henry VIII and Elizabeth I) used both dragon and lion figures to hold the shield in its coat of arms.

Of the thirteen large English warships that were afloat at the beginning of the 16th Century, five still had dragons as figureheads, five had lions and three had other animals. From then on the dragon was seen less and less, and by about 1750 the lion was the dominant figurehead on the warships of all sea powers.

The figurehead lion was regarded as a symbol of the speedy and courageous attacker, it embodied characteristics that were also ascribed to the ship. At the same time though, it embodied the power of the ruler on whose ship it appeared, as did the lion bearing the shield on the coat of arms.

The earliest example of a lion as a figure at the tip of a *Galion* is seen on the model of a galleon, dating from about 1560, in the Netherlands Maritime Museum in

Amsterdam; and a barely younger lion figure, winged like the St. Mark lion of Venice, is found in a drawing of 1586, presumably by the English shipbuilder Matthew Baker, among the "Fragments of Ancient English Shipwrighty" at the Pepsia Library in Cambridge. A splendid copperplate engraving by Christian Möller, dating from 1600, shows a lavishly decorated 64-gun ship of King Christian IV of Denmark, with a springing lion as its figurehead. The next examples of lion figureheads are seen in a painting attributed to the Hollander Aart Van Antum showing the Spanish defeat at Gibraltar in 1607, a painting by Hendrick Cornelisz Vroom of the departure of the English warship *Prince Royal* for Vlissingen in 1613, and a drawing made by Willem Van de Velde the Elder in 1648, showing the English ship *Antelope* which was built in 1618.

The next known figurehead lion is also the oldest figurehead still existing in its original condition. It is that of the *Wasa*, the flagship of King Gustav Adolf of Sweden which sank at Stockholm on its maiden voyage in 1628. It was raised after 333 years in 1961, and in its restored condition today provides an incomparable display of the shipbuilding art of the Renaissance, particularly of the splendor, the richness of detail and the iconology of the lavish carvings that decorated warships at that time. The lion about to spring forward on the bowsprit was carved of linden wood and gilded, measures four meters long and weighs about 450 kilograms (S-ST-WA-1).

On the warships of royal navies, not only in the Scandinavian states but also in England, France, Portugal, Spain and Naples-Sicily, figurehead lions wore crowns as a rule. In England they followed the pattern of the Edward Crown, the English royal crown preserved in the Tower of London, with lilies and crossed paws as fleurons. A crowned lion of this type, presumably from a shallop built in 1720 (GB-LO-NM-44), is found in the National Maritime Museum in Greenwich.

The prow of a model of a Lübeck warship, dating from 1617, with a seahorse figure; a votive model in the church at Landkirchen, Fehmarn.

 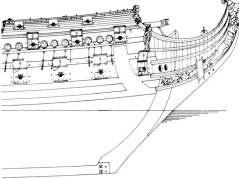

Left: Drawing of the prow of the *Wasa*, based on an official photo from the Sjöhistoriska Museum in Stockholm.

Right: The prow of a model of a Dutch ship of about 1660-1670, formerly in the Maritime Museum of Berlin, drawn by Wolf-Dietrich Wagner.

The Danish Maritime Museum at Kronborg Castle in Helsingör has a drawing of the bow of the Danish East Indiaman *Prints Friedrich* with Swedish inscription and a scale in Swedish feet. The ship is obviously named after the crown prince who became King Frederick V of Denmark in 1746. The figurehead of this Danish ship, obviously built before 1746, also wears—remarkably enough—the English crown. The fact that Frederick's mother was the daughter of a King of England can scarcely have been the reason. The figure measured fourteen feet, or about four meters, from its rearmost claw to its crown, like the Wasa lion which is almost a century older. It is more like the figure on the shipyard model, preserved at Greenwich, of the battleship *Centurion* built in Portsmouth in 1732. And a very similar type, also with the Edward's Crown, is a lion that decorated a well in a farmyard south of Stockholm for many years until the Stockholm Museum of Sea History obtained and restored it in 1930. According to Hanne Poulsen, it came from an East Indiaman built in 1743 (S-ST-SS-7).

The royal figurehead lions were always gilded, while those used on ships in Holland were usually painted red with a yellow or occasionally gilded mane, and wore no crown. In the Rotterdam Maritime Museum *Prins Hendrik* there is a very meticulously water-colored design drawing of the bow of a yacht with such a red Dutch Baroque lion holding a shield, dating from the beginning of the 18th Century. The big red lion in the Maritime Museum at Kronborg Castle too, which was once sawn in half and used to decorate the gate of a Jutland estate, was presumably found on the North Sea shore in the 17th Century and may well have come from a Dutch warship (DK-HE-HS-2).

The figurehead lion of the *Wasa* of 1628 does not wear a crown either, although it adorns what was specifically designated as a *regal ship*. But instead of that, it holds in its paws the crowned coat of arms of its master, King Gustav Adolf of Sweden.

Preserved in their original form are the figurehead lions of the Danish warship *Enigheden* of 1650 at the Orlog Museum of Copenhagen (DK-KH-OR-1), two lions from ships of the first quarter of the 18th Century that stand in front of taverns in Alfriston (GB-AL-SI-1) and Martlesham (GB-MH-RL-1), as well as the lion from a Bavarian elector's pleasure craft of 1769 in the regional museum oat Starnberg am See (D-ST-HM-2). A very impressive later example is the lion figure from the Turkish frigate *Assari i Tewki*, built around 1860 and now privately owned in Germany (D-KI-ST.1).

19

Other Figureheads

The figures on figureheads were not all lions. To be sure, lions still dominated warships until the middle of the 18th Century. And particularly the warships equipped with cannons, the ships of the line, frigates, corvettes and shallops, plus the smaller yachts and pleasure craft of the princes, all had figureheads. But not only were warships armed in those days, so were all larger freighters and the East and West Indiamen that traveled overseas, because of the constant danger of pirates and privateers. Up to the beginning of the 19th Century warships and merchant ships differed primarily in that space for guns and their use was stressed in the former, and space for cargoes in the latter.

Aside from lions, the bow timbers of these ships also bore other animal figures whose typical qualities such as strength, speed or stamina were meant to symbolize the whole ship. Seahorses and dolphins, for example, represented speed, seaworthiness and mobility in battle on the sea, and simultaneously served as protectors of seafarers. The figure of a seahorse, with a horse's body and a fish's tail, for example, decorates the prow of the model of a Lübeck warship of 1617 in the church at Landkirchen on Fehmarn, as well as the stem of a ship model from 1689 in a church in Finström, Finland. The model of an American merchant ship from Newburyport, of about 1760, found in the Peabody Museum in Salem, has a two-headed seahorse as its figurehead. Dolphin bow figures are found, among others, on two surviving princely pleasure craft, namely the luxurious 1732 bark of Frederick, Prince of Wales, in the National Maritime Museum in Greenwich (GB-LO-NM-68) and one of the two pleasure craft in the Stockholm Sea Historical Museum (S-ST-SS-39) built by the renowned shipbuilder Fredrik Henrik af Chapman for King Gustav III of Sweden in 1787. The other royal boat there has a boar's head before its stem (S-ST-SS-38). The pleasure craft used by the Bavarian electors on the Starnberger Sea, as shown in a contemporary watercolor at the Starnberg Regional Museum, used animal figures such as stags, swans and the aforementioned lions as figureheads. The museum possesses the originals of the last two, carved in 1769 (D-ST-HM-1, 2).

Heraldic animals too, such as eagles and mystical griffins (with eagle's head, lion's body and wings) or unicorns (with a horse's body and a long pointed horn on their forehead), symbols of the regal shipowner's person and house, played a role as figureheads. For example, the imperial eagle adorned the bow of the Danube ship that brought Kaiser Leopold I back to his capital from Linz after the Turks were driven away from Vienna in 1683. (A-LI-OL-1).

Among these heraldic figures we can also include the wild man that holds such shields as that of the royal Danish coat of arms and is found, for example, on the prow of a model ship from Holland, dating from the first half of the 18th Century and is seen in the Amsterdam Maritime Museum. The ancient figure of Hercules and those of the wild men from Germanic mythology represented strength and stamina.

Antique gods, saga heroes and rulers had already appeared among the hundreds of rich individual woodcarvings that decorated the great stern surfaces and side galleries

Left: Head from an overseas ship of Holland, from the first half of the 17th Century, found in the former Zuider Zee area; Museum voor Scheepsarcheologie, Ketelhaven.

Right: Head from the Swedish warship *Wasa*, carved in 1628; Statens Sjohistoriska Museum, Wasavarvet, Stockholm.

of warships since the end of the 16th Century. Since the raising and restoration of the *Wasa*, which includes nearly five hundred individual carved figures, and the painstaking scientific study of their iconological system by Hans Soop, it has become clear how greatly humanistic education and the allegorical transmission of ancient concepts to the purposes, qualities and symbolic meaning of warships have determined their decoration. Among the figureheads where the lion had long reigned, though, this first became noticeable only with the coming of Classicism in the last quarter of the 18th Century.

This fondness for figures from Greco-Roman mythology—which lasted through the last wooden ships of the line and frigates of the 19th Century and was still seen around the turn of the last century in countless merchant ships which bore the names of classical gods and heroes—can be traced precisely in its development since enough of the original figures, whose origins are known, still survive from these times. They come from ships with such names as *Apollo, Zeus, Mars, Mercury, Achilles, Andromeda, Venus, Naiad,* and, naturally, *Neptune* and *Poseidon.*

The French in particular used "classic" figureheads quite early, as shown in numerous design drawings dated from since the end of the 17th Century and preserved at the Maritime Museum in Paris. One of the favorite figures from ancient mythology was the goddess of victory, Nike or Victoria. She already appeared, with billowing sails in her outstretched hands, as a figure on ships that are portrayed on Greek coins, as well as on the trunk of a ship monument from Samothrace in Asia Minor, of about 180 B.C., now at the Louvre in Paris. The goddess of victory, holding a laurel wreath high, also decorated the stem of the barge on which Lord Nelson's body was rowed up the Thames in 1805 to be buried in St. Paul's Cathedral. This victory figure is presently in the National Maritime Museum in Greenwich (GB-LO-NM-54).

Among the possessions of the Danish fleet in the Orlogsmuseet of Copenhagen are the wax models of the Danish warships planned (and for the most part built) at the Royal Shipyards between 1711 and 1853. The design drawings of some of them are also preserved at the Federal Archives in Copenhagen. Of these models, 43 in all, twelve figures come from classical mythology, beginning with a Poseidon of 1711 and ending with a naiad figure of 1853.

This model collection is also very informative as to other figureheads used on warships in the 18th and 19th Centuries. At first, from 1725 and 1736, there were two more lions, but then came increasing numbers of figures which, like those from the Greco-Roman mythology, refer directly to the name of the ship, a function that was formerly fulfilled by the figure placed in the center of the stern panel of the richly decorated warships.

Only a very few stern sculptures of the 17th Century that symbolize the name of the ship have survived. In the Sea Historical Museum in Stockholm, for example, there is a life-size mounted figure of King Karl XI, made in 1678; and in the Museum of Hamburg History the more than life-size stern figures from the Hamburg convoy ships *Kaiser Leopoldus Primus* of 1669, with a statue of the Emperor, and *The Admiralty of Hamburg* of 1691, with the colorful, larger-than-life figure of an admiral in a contemporary Baroque uniform, with sword-belt and plumed hat.

Among others, the model collection in Copenhagen includes figureheads that represent districts of the Danish monarchy after which the warships were named: for the ship of the line *Jutland*, a steer with a fish's body (DK-KH-OR-7); and for the ship *Oldenburg* of 1740, the figure of a man wrestling with a lion; plus figures from Nordic mythology representing the names of the ships, such as *Thor* or *Freya*; portrait figures of Danish kings, and an elephant's head from the ship of the line *Elephant*, built in 1741, named after the traditional Danish royal Order of the Elephant (DK-KH-OR-9).

The growing variety of subjects that these examples from the Danish fleet indicate appears also in the figureheads of warships from other lands. In the magazine of the naval shipyard at Karlskrona, the figureheads of the Swedish warships taken out of service since the end of the 18th Century have been preserved. Today they rank among the most important treasures of the maritime museum there. The best examples were created by fleet sculptor Johann Törnström and his son Emanuel. Along with figureheads in Classic style, made for ships built in 1784 and 1789 that embody their names *Försiktigheten* (foresight) and *Dristigheten* (courage)(S-KK-MM-6, 17), there are also figures from the world of classical or Nordic mythology and portrait sculptures of kings.

Figures of the monarchs after whom the ships were named already existed in the 18th Century in the navies of other lands too. The design drawing of the sculptor Caffieri in the Paris Marine Museum, dating from 1758, shows the figurehead of the French ship of the line *Royal Louis*, with a portrait of Louis XV framed by lush tendrils in the transitional style between Rococo and Classicism, and with the whole figure in Roman dress, conforming to the taste of the time. The Swedish King Gustav III, similarly clad in Roman style, is seen as a figurehead in a design drawing, preserved at the Stockholm Sea Historical Museum, for the ship of the line named after him, and made by the renowned shipbuilder Fredrik Henrik af Chapman in 1777.

Right: The bow and figurehead of a model of a ship of the line from Holland, built by the Admiralty of Seeland in 1698, now at the Rijksmuseum in Amsterdam.

Groups of Figures

On horseback, and often life-size, monarchs appeared on figureheads. The figurehead of the *Sovereign of the Seas*, launched in 1637 and the largest British warship up to that time, portrayed King Edgar of Wessex on his horse, with seven vassal kings trodden beneath its hooves. The ship of the line *Naseby*, dating from the Puritan Commonwealth days of 1655, had as its figurehead an equestrian statue of the Lord Protector, Oliver Cromwell, and a guardian angel wearing a laurel wreath. Equestrian figures also adorned the British ship of the line *Prince Royal*, built in 1610 and shown in a painting by the Hollander Hendrick Cornelisz Vroom at the Maritime Museum in Greenwich, and a Spanish ship of the line off Naples in a painting by Abram Willaerts of 1671, also found in Greenwich.

The Saxon King Edgar on horseback with the subordinated vassals at his feet on the *Sovereign of the Seas* is an example of the very lavish figure groups that decorated first-rank British ships of the line from the second third of the 17th Century to the middle of the 18th, while all warships of lesser rank from this period, almost without exception, bore the obligatory crowned lion figures.

Left: King Karl XI of Sweden on horseback, stern figure of the Swedish warship *Carolus XI*, of 1679; Statens Sjöhistoriska Museum, Stockholm.

Right: Prow and figurehead of a model of the British warship *Naseby*, with the Lord Protector, Oliver Cromwell, on horseback, made in 1655; National Maritime Museum, Greenwich.

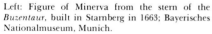

Left: Figure of Minerva from the stern of the *Buzentaur*, built in Starnberg in 1663; Bayerisches Nationalmuseum, Munich.

Right: Stern figure of the Hamburg convoy ship *Die Admiralität von Hamburg,* carved in 1691; Museum vur Hamburgische Geschichte, Hamburg.

The figurehead of the ship of the line *St. Michael* of 1669, of which a contemporary scale model exists in the museum at Greenwich, portrays a double eagle on which two cherubs are riding. It is pulling a triumphal car in which a naked female figure sits. The meaning of this completely gilded group is unclear. The model of the *Royal George* of 1756, also preserved in Greenwich, has a figurehead with two rearing horses with their riders standing beside them, grouped symmetrically around the crowned British coat of arms. One of the most complex compositions of this kind, though, was the group of figures on the figurehead of the *Victory*, which decorated the later flagship of Admiral Nelson from its construction in 1765 to its rebuilding before the battle of Trafalgar in 1805. The original model of this group, made by the sculptor William Savage, is likewise owned by the museum in Greenwich (GB-LO-NM-24).

The instructions of the British Admiralty about the formation of these figurehead groups is still extant. It describes a laurel-wreathed bust of King George with the British coat of arms below it, surrounded by four cherubs representing the four wind directions. Beside it on the starboard side, the crowned Britannia sits before an arch of triumph, her feet on figures representing envy and disharmony, while the figure of Peace holds a laurel wreath and a palm frond over her; the British lion appears behind the triumphal arch, while allegorical figures of the continents of Europe and America carry the base of the triumphal arch on their shoulders, and a genius with a palm frond beside them represents Peace. On the starboard side, similarly positioned, are the figures of the goddess of victory, Victoria, stamping on a five-headed hydra representing Rebellion; beside this is an allegorical figure representing Fame. Here the triumphal arch is supported by the figures of Asia and Africa, and beside them is another genius, this time representing Mathematics and Seafaring, with a symbolic globe and compasses in its hands. This lavish carving measured at least seven meters high, five and a half wide and three and a half deep.

These overloaded Baroque groups of figures, such as sometimes occurred on Danish, Swedish, Spanish and occasionally also on French warships, dominated on the great vessels of the British fleet, until an Admiralty regulation of 1790 strictly limited the luxurious extent of woodcarving. In general too, all these group sculptures (and individual figures too) assumed an almost upright position since the construction of the prow had become steeper and shorter around the middle of the 17th Century. None of them has survived in the original.

Figureheads of the 19th Century

Most of the figureheads still in existence today were made since 1800, and since that date there was scarcely any limit to their subjects. Along with the traditional sculptures of dragons or lions, ancient or Germanic gods and heroes, historic and contemporary monarchs, allegorical figures and those that symbolized countries, states or districts, the many variations eventually included all practical realms of life in their time: a shipowner's wife, children or favorite dog, portraits of office-holding politicians such as Gladstone, Disraeli, Gambetta or Bismarck, to stage stars such as the French mime Talma or the celebrated Swedish singer Jenny Lind.

All of these figureheads can be divided roughly into three groups: those that were created for warships and other state vessels (and usually made traditionally by professional sculptors); those figures carved for larger merchant and passenger vessels, usually owned by important shipping firms (also often made by professional artists); and finally those attached to the bows of thousands of smaller sailing craft, which characterized the scenes of coastal waters and harbors all over the world up to the turn of the century. Most of them were built in shipyards where work was done by hand, and their figureheads were often made, along with the ships themselves, by more-or-less artistically capable ships' carpenters. These objects, which can be seen to a certain degree as a kind of international maritime folklore, form the great majority of the figureheads in museums and private collections today.

Since 1800 complete figures also became rarer; three-quarter, half or one-quarter figures, or even mere busts and heads were preferred, most of them mounted on scroll bases. Here the wealth of subjects seems to have been quite endless.

Often enough a figure was dispensed of entirely and the stem was decorated with scrolls richly adorned with flowers and tendrils. *Krulle,* a word used like the English word "scroll", means "roll, tube, spiral, column or snail" and refers to things like the scrollwork on the neck of a violin. Thus they are sometimes called *fiddleheads,* or more commonly *billetheads,* which means the head or front end of a billet of wood. The spiral scroll crowning the stem sometimes existed even in ancient times. The coiled snake-head of the Oseberg ship was derived from a similar form and, instead of a figure, the model of a Flemish galleon of 1593 at the Naval Museum in Madrid also has a large decorative scroll at the tip of the prow. But only in the 19th Century, after the *Galion* design disappeared, did the scroll become a common, favorite form of stem ornamentation. In many of the great steel windjammers too, such as the five-masted German ship *Preussen* that was built in 1902 at Geestemünde-Bremerhaven, the bow was decorated with a voluminous scroll. Another characteristic of these late sailing ships was the trail boards that were customary in the 19th Century, long boards with colorfully painted or gilded tendrils and leaves in relief carving. They trailed like comets' tails along the woodwork for several meters alongside the figurehead, more or less indicating the lines of the vanished *Galion* on the prow of the clipper.

The sort of figureheads on warships in the 19th Century turned out to be nothing new in iconological terms. A good number of these carvings from the last wooden warships in world history, often of high artistic quality, still exist in naval depots or national maritime museums, including those in Paris, Toulon, Lisbon, Athens, Istanbul, Rotterdam, Leningrad, Karlskrona, Copenhagen, London, Portsmouth,, Dresden, Flensburg, Bremerhaven, Annapolis, Newport News and Vienna.

When the forward-sweeping clipper bow became established in the early 19th Century, the figures—supported by a kneelike wooden frame—were attached to the prow below the bowsprit, either directly or on a base. The busts and half-figures thus stood almost vertical on their scrolls; the full and three-quarter figures, on the other hand, followed the inclination of the bowsprit and thus gained a diagonal position rather like the figures at the tip of the flat *Galion* of the early 17th Century. These figures, looking over the water into the distance from their diagonal position under the bowsprit, set the familiar pattern for figureheads during the last century, just as they decorate the bows of the last great sailing school ships still afloat today.

Bow with figurehead of a British ship off Liverpool, painting by Robert Salmon, 1804, in the National Maritime Museum, Grenwich.

Fleet Sculptors

The technique of figurehead carving was really nothing more than the formerly widespread technique of woodcarving in general. It should not be forgotten that everywhere in Europe except in the south, and likewise in North America, houses were built primarily of wood until into the 19th Century, and thus the work of the carpenter ranked well above that of the bricklayer or stone mason. In shipbuilding, until iron and later steel construction prevailed at the latter half of the 19th Century, wood was used without exception. Ships' carpenters, rather than riveters and welders, dominated the work at the shipyards.

As related as the techniques of carpentry and design methods in house- and shipbuilding were, so too were their decorative and artistic adornments: the carved friezes, rosettes, pedestals and figures on half-timbered houses from the Gothic age to the Classical, on the one hand; and on the other, the similar ornamentation on the bows and sterns of the wooden ships of those times. And as with all those works of art destined for dry land, there were also three levels of those used aboard ships: that of courtly-academic art, that of the upper bourgeoisie, and the so-called folk art, produced more by artisans than by artists.

The shipbuilders and figurehead carvers were no less capable or respected than their colleagues who created figures for castles, churches or city halls. In fact, in the seaport towns it was usually the same artists and workshops that provided, for example, carved altars for churches and sculptures for ships. An example would be Christian Precht, born in Bremen and settled in Hamburg, who created not only works for the churches of St. Catherine and St. James there, but also a carved stone relief for the altar of the church of St. Cosmas in Stade and the bow and stern figures of the two convoy ships *Wapen von Hamburg* built in 1668 and 1686. He also created the 1688 portrait figure of Kaiser Leopold I, still preserved at the Museum of Hamburg History, for the convoy ship named after him. The third ship with the name of *Wapen von Hamburg*, commissioned in 1720, carried a figurehead and stern figures made by the sculptor Johann Christoffer von der Heyde, who carved the Baroque high altar of St. Peter's Church in Hamburg a few years later.

The still inadequate research into the art of woodcarving in shipbuilding, and thus of the history of figurehead carving, makes it inevitable that less is known of their production than that of the other realms of sculpture. Only a few limited areas have been researched thoroughly, thanks to the work of M. V. Brewington on the North American shipbuilders, of Hanne Poulsen on Danish figureheads, with much biographical information about their carvers; and particularly the pioneering work of Hans Soop, who has researched the more than six hundred individual pieces of carving on the *Wasa* and their iconological, artistic and social historical background.

Though somewhat less lavishly, the *Wasa* and the other great *royal* warships of the time were decorated with similar ornamental carvings as that of the famous *Sovereign of the Seas*, the largest and most elegant sailing ship in the world up to its time which King Charles I of England had had built and decorated with hundreds of gilded figures and other ornamental sculptures according to a detailed plan made by his court painter--the famous Flemish student of Rubens, Anthony Van Dyck. Only on the *Wasa*, though, were these carvings preserved in their original form, along with the great lion figurehead (S-ST-WA-1).

Hans Soop has identified the artists who created them. The most significant and productive of them, who probably planned the entire program using pattern books and ornamental designs from Holland, was Mårten Redtmer. He was presumably born in Germany or The Netherlands and the most highly respected sculptor in the royal residence and seaport city of Stockholm at that time. Among his works are organ carvings and tombs of noteworthy quality, preserved in Swedish churches. Along with him, the sculpturing work for the *Wasa* was entrusted to the sculptors Hans Clausink and Johan Thesson. The different styles of the three artists can be recognized with considerable certainty in the individual sculptures. The figurehead lion was quite obviously carved by Master Redtmer himself.

It appears that the sculptors worked under exclusive contracts to the royal shipyards in Stockholm while they ornamented the *Wasa*, though it is not likely that one or another of them held an official position as fleet sculptor. The position of admiralty sculptor did exist later at the naval shipyard in Karlskrona, where most Swedish warships were built since the end of the 17th Century. Hindrik Schütz, who supplied the great equestrian figure of King Karl IX for the stern of the ship named after him in 1678, was the first to hold office there, retaining it until 1701 when the naval sculptor Johann Jakob Walldau succeed him. After the middle of the century, the obviously untalented Niklas Ekekrantz worked as admiralty sculptor in Karlskrona; in the opinion of the shipyard supervisor at the time, his figurehead lions looked like dogs and his gods like aquatic ghosts. He was succeeded in 1781 by Johan Törnström of Stockholm, who was a protege of the famous shipwright Fredrik Henrik af Chapman, who had become the leader of the Karlskrona shipyard the previous year. At the Djugård shipyard in Stockholm, where Chapman had built the East Indiaman *King Gustav II* and the royal yacht *Amphion*, Törnström had worked on carvings for these ships as an assistant to the sculptor Jean Baptiste Masreliez. Along with his colleague C. P. Gerdes, who lived on the shipyard premises, Törnström had also done work at the castle in Stockholm. The figurehead for the *Amphion* was made by Törnström's Stockholm colleague Per Ljung, who was about the same age. At this time the art of sculpture in Sweden was strongly influenced by Johan Tobias Sergel, Sweden's most important artist in this field. He was born in Stockholm in 1740 and returned in 1778 from a twelve-year stay in Rome, where he had devoted himself completely to Classicism. He worked for the court in Stockholm and made, among other things, wax models and designs for figureheads.

Törnström, who was born in 1743 and had originally been a furniture carver, practiced his art for the navy at Karlskrona until 1825. The best of his figureheads, which he made chiefly for the Swedish warships designed by Chapman, certainly show the influence of Sergel's strict Classicism. They are of high artistic quality and can still be seen in the shipyard museum at Karlskrona today. Johan Törnström's son Emanuel, who learned the art in his father's studio, followed him in office and worked at it until he died in 1883, when the end of figurehead production for wooden sailing warships was not far off. After Emanuel, L. Nordin was the last admiralty sculptor at Karlskrona. He already created figureheads for steamships, the last of them a bust of St. Eric for the ship of the line *Stockholm* in 1856. After that the Swedish Navy had their figureheads made by well-known Stockholm sculptors; in 1862 Henrik Nerpin carved that of the steam frigate *Vanadis* (S-ST-SM-37), and Carl August Sundwall that of the steam frigate *Saga* (S-KK-MM-11) in 1878.

In Denmark, official *master sculptors of the fleet* are documented from 1652 on. From 1669 to 1694 Tyge Larsen held this office; his father Lars Worm (or Lauritz Hansen Worm) had also been a sculptor and probably worked for the fleet. Larsen also created carvings for new Danish warships built in Oslo. In addition to him, the naval shipyard employed four other sculptors as masters. Instructions from King Frederick

Left: Design drawing by F. C. Willerup for the figurehead of the Danish warship *Neptunus* of 1789; Handels- og Söfartsmuseet Helsingör.

Right: Design drawing by F. C. Willerup for the figurehead of a Danish warship, showing Jupiter upon an eagle, circa 1790; Handels- og Söfartsmuseet Helsingör.

II to Larsen, dating from about 1670 and including precise descriptions of details to be carved for the warship *Flyende Fisk,* have been preserved. A fish on a scroll was prescribed as the figurehead.

Wax models of later figureheads for the Danish Navy exist in the Orlogsmuseet in Copenhagen, the earliest for the ship *Laaland* of 1711 (DK-KH-OR-3), the last dating from 1886 and made for the corvette *Dagmar,* built in 1861 (DK-KH-OR-48).

Similar models, made for Dutch warships from the late 18th to the mid-19th Century, are owned by the Rijksmuseum in Amsterdam as well as the Maritime Museum in Rotterdam. One of these was made for the corvette *Ajax* (NL-RO-MA-21), built in 1832; its original, portraying a Roman warrior, is in the Maritime Museum at Amsterdam. This excellent sculpture, originally painted white, was somewhat spoiled by being painted in bright colors some years ago (NL-AM-RS-5).

The Sea History Museum in Stockholm still has L. Nordin's model of his figurehead of St. Eric for the ship of the line *Stockholm* (S-ST-SS-40). And mention has already been made of the model group in the museum at Greenwich, which sculptor William Savage made in 1765 at the naval shipyards in Chatham for the stem of the *Victory* (GB-LO-NM-24).

The building commissions of the fleets, often in their king's presence, used to use such models to decide on the figureheads of planned ships. It is known that the Danish models, like the many design drawings in the royal archives at Copenhagen, were made by early fleet sculptors themselves.

Since 1734 Just Wiedewelt, son of a Danish court architect who came from the Meissen area and had built Frederiksborg Castle, was master sculptor at the royal fleet shipyard at Christiansholm and simultaneously professor and director of the sculpture class at the Copenhagen Academy of Art. From 1698 to 1715 he had been in Paris, and the French influence in his works is obvious, as shown in the figurehead models for the ships of the line *Oldenburg* of 1740 (DK-KH-OR-8) and *Elephanten* of 1741 (DK-KH-OR-9).

After Wiedewelt's death in 1757, he was succeeded in office by Simon Carl Stanley, royal court sculptor and, since 1752, professor at the Academy of Art. He had studied in Germany and Holland and spent twenty years in England, particularly making tombs and sculptured decorations for the country seats of the higher nobility, before beginning to work at the fleet shipyards in Copenhagen in 1750. When he died in 1761, Chr. Jacobsen Mollerup succeeded him as master sculptor of the fleet; his successor in the master's office, F. C. Willerup, worked under him from 1776 on. The latter was a student of Just Wiedewelt's son, Professor Johannes Wiedewelt, who was Denmark's leading sculptor at that time, at the Copenhagen Academy. Like his Swedish contemporary Johan Törnström, Willerup became the most renowned figurehead carver in his country. He did not make wax models, but rather many carefully executed design drawings, which are preserved at the Trade and Maritime Museum in Kronborg Castle today. When he retired at the age of seventy-four in 1816, the office of master sculptor of the Danish fleet was abolished.

Since then, figureheads and other carvings for ships were made at the shipyards by artisan woodcarvers to designs that were originally provided by the renowned painter and academy professor Christoffer Wilhelm Eckersberg, as well as by the sculptor H. W. Bissen and the shipyard designer Johan Daniel Petersen, who worked at the shipyard as a sculptor along with the artisans.

Some of Eckersberg's design drawings made between 1819 and 1824 have been preserved at the Orlogsmuseum, as have a series of wax models made according to his designs; the only figure that exists is the *Dronning Marie*, owned by the Copenhagen Fleet Station at Christiansholm (DK-KH-FL-1). Eckersberg, born near Flensburg in 1783, was a famous portrait and maritime painter. He was a friend to the fleet and its officers, as well as to the designers at the fleet shipyard, especially Patersen.

The names of most of the artisan sculptors employed at the shipyards, who produced figureheads and other carvings (Eckersberg's, Bissen's and Petersen's drawings, among others), are still known. In 1821 the leader was Henrik Knudsen Trane, who had replaced Peter Rasmus Vermundsen on his death in 1819, plus Jacob Peter Holm, Ditlev Anthon Brokman and apprentices Johann Peter Helt and Henrik Julius Móen. The last founded his own successful studio in 1842, at which many figureheads for Danish merchant ships were produced.

The cooperation between the painter Eckersberg, the sculptor Bissen and the shipbuilder Petersen lasted until Petersen died in 1848. In the last years of his life he was helped by his son, Julius Magnus Petersen, who then provided a series of design drawings for the figureheads of Danish warships. Included were the corvette *Heimdal* in 1848 and the frigates *Niels Juel* and *Jylland*, launched in 1855 and 1860 respectively, which fought against the Austrians and Prussians in the sea battle off Helgoland in 1864. The wax model for the figurehead of the *Heimdal* is in the Orlogsmuseet in Copenhagen (DK-KH-OR-46), the figure owned by the fleet station there (DK-KH-FL-7). The figure from the *Niels Juel* is also preserved at the fleet station (DK-KH-FL-7), the model of that of the *Jylland* is at the Orlogsmuseum (DK-KH-OR-47), while its figure still adorns the bow of the ship which is preserved in the harbor of Ebeltoft (D-EB-EK-1).

Among the last figureheads made for 19th Century Danish warships is that of the screw corvette *Dagmar*, carved in 1886 by sculptor Ulrik Björn after a model by architect Vilhelm Dahlerup. This model—the last of the Danish naval collection preserved in the Orlogsmuseum—still exists (DK-KH-OR-48), and the figure itself is still at the Copenhagen Fleet Station (DK-KH-FL-6).

Left: Port-side figure from a Venetian galley of the end of the 17th Century; Museo Storico Navale, Venice.

Right: Model of the royal galley of Louis XIV, *La Réale*, with sculptures carved by Pierre Puget in 1690' Musée de la Marine, Paris.

In France as well as Denmark and Sweden, outstanding sculptors, often simultaneously working for the court, were contracted to produce sculptured ornaments for warships. When the subsequent Copenhagen fleet sculptor Just Wiedewelt was active in Paris between 1698 and 1715, French Baroque sculpture was at its zenith. The *Sun King* Louis XIV, who reigned from 1643 to 1715, had drawn a great number of outstanding artists and artisans to his court, especially for the construction of his splended Palace of Versailles. Among the sculptors who worked on the palace and gardens of Versailles was Philippe Caffieri, who was born in Rome in 1634. Between 1676 and 1680 he carved the ornamental designs and figures for the gondolas and ornate barks of the palace waters. From 1687 to 1714 Caffieri worked as a fleet sculptor at the naval shipyard in Dunkerque and was responsible for decorating the warships built there. In 1714 his son François-Charles Caffieri, who was born in 1667 and had already assisted his father at Versailles, took over the position at Dunkerque, but assumed the same office at the naval shipyard in Brest as early as 1717, while his son Charles Philippe Caffieri (Philippe's grandson) succeeded him at Dunkerque. In 1729 the latter took over the position at Brest on his father's death, holding it until his own death in 1766. It can be assumed that the Caffieris, who held the position of fleet sculptors for almost eighty years, designed and, to some extent, also carved the decorations for most of the French warships built at Dunkerque or Brest themselves, including the figureheads. The Paris Marine Museum preserves numerous design drawings by François-Charles and his son Charles Philippe, made between 1721 and 1765.

At Toulon, the most important Mediterranean base of the French fleet, Pierre Puget was personally appointed by Louis XIV as the master of the carving workshops of the royal naval shipyard from 1668 to 1679. He was born in Marseilles in 1620, learned woodcarving from the galley builder Jean Roman, was trained as a painter in Florence and Rome, and then won considerable fame as a sculptor in Toulon, Marseilles, Paris and Genoa. The male caryatids he carved in stone in 1657 still stand in front of the Toulon city hall, his marble statue of Hercules is in the Louvre, and in the Paris

33

Marine Museum is the decorative figure of Louis XIV's Mediterranean galley *La Réale* of 1690, along with two gilded stern figures that rank among the masterworks of Baroque plastic art.

The court painter Charles Lebrun, born in 1617 and a founder and director of the Paris Academy of Art, was responsible for the designing and production of ornamentation for all warships under Louis XIV's Minister Colbert, the energetic promoter of French fleet construction. Puget and Philippe Caffieri obviously received their positions because of Lebrun's recommendation. His successor was Jean Bérain who, like Philippe Caffieri, had taken part in the decoration of Versailles at an early age as a designer for furniture and commercial art. In the Paris Musée de la Marine there are also many of his designs for figureheads, including one of 1690 for the ship of the line *Le Brillant*. Philippe Caffieri executed it. For the ship of the line *Soleil Royal*, also built in 1690, the court sculptor Coysevox, born in 1640 and also one of the chief artists to work at Versailles, created the sculptured decorations.

From 1731 to 1760 Jean Ange Maucord, a student of court sculptor B. Marrot at Cavaillon in the Provence, was master sculptor for the fleet at Toulon. In addition to carvings for the warships built at the royal shipyard, he also created tombs and, in 1738, the statue of Minerva for the Porte d'Arsenal, built in Toulon to his design.

His successor and also the sculpture teacher at the naval school of the arsenal was named Gibert, and he in turn was followed in 1792 by his student Jacques Felix Brun, who was born in Toulon in 1763. He held the office until his death in 1831. The decoration for the ship of the line *Montebello*, built in 1812 with a figurehead of Hercules, and for *Le Souverain* of 1819, with a figure of King Louis VXIII, were made by him. For the staircase of the naval hospital in Toulon he created the stone statues of the French kings Henri IV and Louis XIV.

Though Charles I's court painter Anthony Van Dyck had provided the plans and drawings for the decoration of the *Sovereign of the Seas*, it was the Dutch nautical painter Willem Van de Velde and his identically named son who worked at the court and for the fleet in London since 1674, under contract from Charles II. Both ranked among the most prominent sea and ship painters in the history of art. Their paintings have portrayed numerous sea battles and seaport scenes, with detailed reproductions of ships. Many of their drawings also show details of design and decorative figures; there exists, among others, a sketch by Willem Van de Velde the Younger showing the figurehead of the ship of the line *St. Michael*, built in 1669. The accurate pictures and drawings of the Van de Veldes rank among the most important documents that provide information on ship decorations, particularly figureheads, during the latter half of the 17th Century.

Unlike Sweden, Denmark and France, little is known of the artists in England who were given the job of designing and executing sculptured works. The creator of the great group figure for the *Victory*, built in 1765, has already been mentioned--William Savage, who obviously worked officially as fleet sculptor for the royal shipyards in Chatham.

In about 1800 the British Admiralty ordered that drawing and painting instruction should be offered within the framework of officer training at the Naval College in Portsmouth. The painter Richard Livesay, student of the American-born director of the London Academy, Benjamin West, was named to be the first teacher. In 1811 John Christian Schetky, a friend of the famous nautical painter William Turner, joined him. In a special upper-level class, shipbuilding trainees received instruction in drawing, obviously with the intention of teaching them to make designs for figureheads. Nothing is known of the success of this course, which existed for only a short time. In any case, the execution of woodcarving for English warships in the 19th Century appears to have been less the work of official fleet sculptors than of independent artists. For example, the figurehead for the *Warrior* of 1860, the first British armored ship, which portrayed a bearded ancient warrior, was carved by a member of the Hellyer family of sculptors that produced a number of figures for British warships and merchant ships around the middle of the 19th Century. A

Pair of stern figures from the French warship *Fontenoy*, 18th Century; Musée des Beaux-Arts, Boulogne-sur-Mer.

member of the Hellyer family, living in Blackwell, carved the figure of Nannie the witch in her short gown for the tea clipper *Cutty Sark* (GB-LO-CS.1) in 1869; the ship is now docked at Greenwich as a museum ship.

The creation of an American naval fleet began in 1775 during the American war of independence against Britain. From the start, native artists provided the decorations; there were no officially appointed sculptors for the American fleet. From about 1735 to 1830, members of the Skillin family worked as figurehead carvers in Boston, New York and Philadelphia. The studio of John Skillin, born in 1746, and his brother Simeon provided a carved Roman warrior in 1777 for the figurehead of the *Confederacy*, and the third brother, Samuel, carved a nymph for the brigantine *Convention*. The first figurehead for the frigate *Constitution*, now preserved at Boston harbor, was a

35

Hercules made by John and Simeon Skillin to a design of the sculptor William Rusk. What they portrayed was not recorded. In 1804 it was destroyed in a collision and replaced by a scroll. For a time the *Constitution* also had figures of President Andrew Jackson, the first of them carved in 1834 by Laban S. Beecher of Wisconsin and now owned by the Museum of the City of New York (USA-NY-MC-3). The second, now at the Naval Academy in Annapolis (USA-AP-OS-3), was produced in 1848 by the ship sculpture firm of J. D. and W. H. Fowle, founded in 1807 by the talented Bostonian figurehead sculptor Isaac Fowle.

William Rusk, born in 1756 and the son of a Philadelphia shipbuilder, was one of America's most prominent ship sculptors. He studied with the carver Edward Cutbush, who came from England and worked in Philadelphia from 1770 to 1790, and founded his own studio there. Undoubtedly inspired by the marble busts of George Washington and Benjamin Franklin that the famed French sculptor Jean Antoine Houdon had created while in America in 1785, he carved a bust of Benjamin Franklin in 1815 that served as the figurehead of the ship of the line named after Franklin and is now owned by the Naval Academy at Annapolis (USA-AP-US-1).

A friend of Rusk was the Bostonian carver Solomon Willard, born in 1783, who created, among others, the portrait bust of George Washington as the figurehead of the frigate *Washington,* built in Portsmouth, New Hampshire in 1816; the bust is preserved at Annapolis now (USA-AP-US-6). After that, Willard worked for a time in Baltimore, but until his death in 1861 he worked generally as a stone sculptor.

The Peabody Museum in Salem owns a bust of Hercules that the New York studio of Dodge & Sharpe created in 1820 for the frigate *Ohio* (USA-SE-PE-26). It was probably carved by the founder of the firm, the New York shipbuilder's son Jeremiah Dodge, who worked in New York since about 1804 and also had other partners during his lifetime. His son Charles J. Dodge kept his father's firm in business until 1858.

The Mariners Museum in Newport News owns one of the finest and most unusual of all figureheads: the gigantic eagle that adorned the bow of the American warship *Lancaster* since 1875. This work, made of several pieces joined together, was created by the sculptor John Bellamy, born in 1836, who had been an art student in New York and then studied with the Bostonian ship sculptor Laban S. Beecher. Bellamy worked at the U.S. Naval Shipyard in Portsmouth until 1902.

No fleet sculptors' names are known from Holland, where the ship sculptors organized a guild quite early, from Spain, Portugal or Italy. Nor do we know the names of the sculptors who carved the figureheads that adorned the ships of the Prussian and later Imperial German Navy in the 19th Century and are now preserved in the German Maritime Museum in Bremerhaven, the Army Museum in Dresden, or the Naval School at Mürwik. Nor are the names known of those who carved the figureheads of the 19th-Century Austro-Hungarian warships at the Museum of Military History in Vienna, the Greek examples at the Maritime Museum in Piraeus, and the Turkish ones in the Marine Museum at Istanbul. On the other hand, it is known that two figureheads of mid-19th-Century Russian warships at the Marine Museum in Leningrad were carved by Mikerskik and P. K. Klodd (SU-CH-MF-1, 2).

Right: Port stern figure of the pleasure craft of Frederick, Prince of Wales, carved in 1732 by James Richard; National Maritime Museum, Greenwich.

Court Sculptors and Their Work on Royal Pleasure Craft

The display of splendor and the resulting demand for every kind of art and artisanship at the court of Louis XIV, which the royal courts all over Europe soon competed to equal, also affected the use of pleasure craft and the holding of aquatic festivals, a tradition that went back to old Venice. Following the examples of the lavish gondolas and pleasure boats that the Sun King had made for festivities on the waters in the park at Versailles—the Bassin d'Apollon and the Canal de Versailles—and decorated with woodcarvings by Philippe Caffieri, other ornate oar-driven boats from the size of Venetian gondolas to that of small galleys were soon floating on the waters in the vicinity of other European residences. Such ornate craft, many of which were manned by forty oarsmen and thus amounted to very fast *travel boats* for rulers and courtiers, have endured to this day in Lisbon, Aranjuez, London, Stockholm, Paris, the Saxon castle of Pillnitz on the Elbe and in Starnberg, where the Bavarian electoral princes held their aquatic festivals.

Here, in fact, shipbuilders from Venice, using the Venetian state galley as a model (the Bucintoro that was overloaded with the most lavish gilded woodcarving), built a Bavarian *Buzentaur* more than thirty meters long. The sculptors Balthasar Ableitner, Thobias Baader, Johann Bader, Matthias Schutz, Matthias Stainhart and the latter's son Joseph provided the sculptures, some of which are still extant in private ownership or at the Munich National Museum. There too, a colorful wooden sculpture of a nymph is preserved, made scarcely later than 1700, that is presumably a relic and perhaps even a figurehead of one of the smaller pleasure boats that accompanied the princely galley (D-MU-BN-1). The Starnberg Buzentaur existed from 1663 until it was broken up in the middle of the 18th Century.

For three small pleasure craft made in 1769, the Munich court sculptor Johann Strauss was paid 150 Gulden to produce the figureheads, of which a lion and a swan still exist in the Starnberg Regional Museum (D-ST-HM-1, 2). A portrait bust of Queen Caroline of Bavaria, also preserved there, decorated the bow of the pleasure boat named after her in the Biedermeier era and was probably made by the classic sculptor Ludwig Schwantaler, who worked for the court in Munich (D-ST-HM-3). And the pleasure boat completed in 1830 in which King Ludwig I had himself and his favorite Lola Montez rowed around the Starnberger Sea is still at the Regional Museum. The prow is decorated with a dolphin with its tailfins raised high (D-ST-HM-4).

The opulent woodcarving for the pleasure bark of Prince Frederick of Wales, preserved at the museum in Greenwich, was made by the English court sculptor James Richard in 1732 and features the bow figure of a dolphin (GB-LO-NM-68). Unknown, though, are the artists who made the simpler ornaments for the other two surviving royal oar-driven shallops; the state boat of Charles II of England, dating from about 1670, at the Victory Museum in Portsmouth; and the shallop preserved in the museum at Greenwich which William II had made for his wife Queen Mary II. The decorations, including the figureheads of a boar and a dolphin for the two pleasure

Decorations from the pleasure craft *Caroline* of Queen Caroline of Bavaria, presumably carved by Ludwig Schwanthaler, early 19th Century, colored; Bavarian National Museum, Munich.

boats of King Gustav III, built by Chapman in 1787 in Stockholm and now in the Maritime Museum there, were made by the royal fleet sculptor Johan Törnström (S-ST-SS-38, 39). And the two pleasure boats preserved in the Paris Marine Museum, that of Queen Marie Antoinette of 1777 and that of Emperor Napoleon of 1811, are decorated with high-quality ornamental figures and other carvings. The figurehead of Marie Antoinette's *Marie-Thérèse* is a buxom siren (F-PA-MM-3), while that of Napoleon's boat is a figure of Neptune made by the Antwerp sculptor Van Petersen (F-PA-MM-2). This Van Petersen may be identical to Peters, the Antwerp *Commandeur der beeldhouwers,* who likewise supplied a Neptune figure, drawn through the waves by three seahorses, to adorn the bow of the state shallop of King Willem I of The Netherlands. The shallop, with its completely gilded group of figures, now belongs to the Netherlands Naval Station at Den Helder and was last used in 1954 for a state visit of the King of Norway.

Further examples of the high quality that characterized the decoration of such craft are: the six ornate boats of Portuguese kings at the Marine Museum in Lisbon, made between 1728 and 1831 and featuring gilded carved decorations by artists Silvestre de Faria (1753), Manuel Vieira and his student Joaquim José de Barros Labarâo (1780), Manuel da Fonseca Pinto Carneiro (1831) (P-LI-MM-8-13); the still existing and similarly lavishly decorated pleasure craft in the palace of Aranjuez near Madrid, on whose park waters the Spanish kings used to hold aquatic festivals in the Versailles manner; and the Elbe gondola of the Saxon Elector and later King Friedrich August I, dating from 1790 and featuring the figurehead of a river god ostensibly sculpted by a Venetian gondola builder, and now preserved at Pillnitz Castle (DDR-PI-SC-1).

This excursion into court pleasure-craft travel from the Baroque to the Biedermeier era shows how natural it was for sculptors who worked for royalty, from Mårten Redtmer and Pierre Puget to Johannes Tornström and Ludwig Schwanthaler, to create the decorations for their ships too. Since there is no completely preserved original large ship other than the *Wasa,* the approximately twenty remaining pleasure boats are all the more important as examples of authentic historical material.

Previous page: Figure of a nymph, perhaps a figurehead, presumably from a royal Bavarian pleasure craft, colored, circa 1700; Bavarian National Museum, Munich.

40

Independent Figurehead Carvers

The Danish writer Hans Christian Andersen tells in the fairy tale *Holger Danske* of a figurehead sculptor to whom he gave features of his own grandfather who had been such a carver, but also features of the father of his friend—the classic sculptor Bertel Thorvaldsen. Gotskalk Thorvaldsen, who came to Copenhagen from Iceland around 1760, had studied woodcarving there with Peder Pedersen Leed, a wood sculptor who worked for the Danish fleet and later worked as an independent artisan. Bertel, who was born in 1768, had helped his father in his studio as a boy while he was still attending the Copenhagen Art Academy. His teachers at the Academy were Professor Stanley, also a fleet architect, and the Danish sculptor Johannes Wiedewelt—the son of fleet architect Just Wiedewelt, who had been trained in Paris. Even after he was world-famous and lived in Rome, Bertel Thorvaldsen still sent his father designs for figureheads.

Such sculptors' studios that worked mainly on decorations for ships but also created other secular and sacred works, from gravestones to carousel figures, existed in all major seaports in the days of wooden sailing ships. In addition, the larger private shipbuilding firms, especially in the 19th Century, employed their own ship sculptors and figurehead carvers.

Christian Precht and Johann Christoffer von der Heyde, who provided the Baroque sculptures for the Hamburg convoy ships, and perhaps the sculptor Damian Forment too, who made two figures of saints for Spanish warships in Barcelona in 1504, are early examples of the independent masters of sculpting studios in the seaport towns at which most of the 19th-Century figureheads still in existence were made. Thanks to the research of Brewington and Poulsen, more precise information is at hand only from Denmark and North America, and the following data is based on their researches.

The Copenhagen shipbuilder E. P. Bonnesen often supplied his customers with plans for the ships they ordered plus several of his own drawings of figureheads to choose from. A series of such designs from between 1836 and 1852 can be seen at the Trade and Maritime Museum at Helsingör. This museum also owns several contemporary photographs of figureheads that Heinrich Julius Moen (already mentioned as a student of the fleet sculpture studio), and his son William Edelhardt carved in the Fifties, Sixties and Seventies of the 19th Century. William Edelhardt Moen attended the Copenhagen Academy and was trained as a sculptor before working in his father's studio. From 1861 to 1864 he pursued his calling in Apenrade, then returned to Copenhagen, where his father died in 1881. The son lived and worked in the country in northern Seeland in his later years.

Other Danish figurehead carvers whose names we know were the master carpenter Gebhardt, in Apenrade circa 1830; Fr. Chr. Jörgensen, a student of the elder Moen in Copenhagen; Schroder, who worked at Middelfart around 1860; and C. Stephensen, who carved the figurehead of the yacht *Standart*, built in Copenhagen in 1895 for the last Russian Tsar, Nicholas II.

In twentieth century Denmark, the sculptor Emil Clemmensen (1931 for the still-active royal yacht *Dannebrog*) and A. Syberg Bang (1933 for the sail school ship *Danmark*, also still afloat) created figureheads (DK-KH-DI-1).

Bow of the British East Indiaman *Asia*, with prow and portrait bust as figurehead, off Hong Kong in 1836; painting by John Huggins; National Maritime Museum, Greenwich.

Brewington has recorded the names of over 250 sculptors and firms that produced decorations for ships, and particularly figureheads, in some fifty American seaports in the states of Connecticut, California, Louisiana, Maine, Maryland, Massachusetts, Michigan, New Hampshire, New York, Pennsylvania, Rhode Island, South Carolina, Virginia and Wisconsin, plus the District of Columbia and the Canadian provinces of New Brunswick and Quebec. The most important ports were Baltimore, Boston, Salem, Portsmouth (New Hampshire), New York, Philadelphia, Charleston and San Francisco.

Other than the sculptors already noted as having supplied ships of the American fleet, those who stand out particularly include Samuel McIntire, born in Salem in 1757, by whom the Peabody Museum there has the figure of a woman (USA-SE-Pe-4); the Irishman John W. Mason, active in Boston since about 1838, many of whose design drawings for figureheads are also preserved at the Peabody Museum; C. A. L. Sampson, who worked in Boston in 1847 and later in Bath, Maine, who created the figureheads of the *Western Belle* of 1876 and the *Belle of Bath* in 1877, both now in the Peabody Museum; Edbury Hatch, who worked in Damiriscotta, Maine since 1870, many of whose designs for figureheads are owned by Brewington; and Edward Bell Lovejoy, born in San Francisco in 1857 and active there, presumably as California's last figurehead carver, until his death in 1917. The most noteworthy Canadian was probably the Scottish-born John Rogerson, who studied in Boston from, among others, John D. Fowle (the son of Isaac Fowle), before he opened his own studio in St. John, New Brunswick and ran it until 1887. Figures made by him are found in the Museum of New Brunswick, the Mariners Museum in Newport News, and the Addison Gallery in Andover (USA-AN-AD-1).

Among others, working as independent figurehead carvers in Sweden were Peter M. Hagman in Kalmar around 1770, and in the 19th Century the already mentioned Henrik Nerpin and Carl August Sundwall in Stockholm. In Finland, Erkki Annanpoika worked at Pretarsaari around 1838-39, and in Germany the studio of the Klindworth brothers, open for many decades in Blankenese, provided numerous figureheads to Hamburg shipyards since 1876; many of their drawings are now in the

Bow of the British clipper *Barossa* with figurehead and trail boards, 1874; painting by F. Tudgay, National Maritime Museum, Greenwich.

Altona Museum. In Germany there were the studios of Heinrich Köster in Cranz on the Elbe since 1865 and that of Robert Rüsch in Cuxhaven, one of the last (until 1917) practitioners of the art in Germany, as was Wilhelm Wittland of Bremerhaven. It was Wittland who, just after the turn of the century, carved the figureheads or scrolls for the great steel five-masters *Potosi, Preussen* and *R. C. Rickmers*, among others, as well as the portrait figure of Grand Duke Friedrich August of Oldenburg for the German school ship named after him in 1914. This ship is now the Norwegian *Statsraad Lehmkuhl.*

The art effectively ended all over the world with the advent of World War I. Yet in recent years several artists, mostly self-taught, on their own and without having learned the art in old-style studios, have specialized in carving figureheads. Jack Whitehead and Norman Gaches, who work on the Isle of Wight, might be cited; they have equipped a number of sailing yachts in various countries and the British school ships *Sir Winston Churchill* and *Royalist* with figureheads (GB-LO-SC-1) and provided all the decorative sculpture for the reproductions of historic ships such as Sir Francis Drake's *Golden Hinde* (US-SG—GH-1). In addition, they have restored old figures including those of the Cutty Sark Collection in Greenwich. In 1972 they took their studio to the Olympia Exposition in Kiel, where the German Bernd Alm was inspired by them to make a profession of carving figureheads. For the German Maritime Museum in Bremerhaven he has made an outstanding replica of the lost figurehead of the five-masted bark *R. C. Rickmers,* one of the last great sailing cargo ships, which sank in the Irish Sea in 1917. In England, Charles Moore is still active as a figurehead carver in Truro, and in America, Ramon Parga is working in Salem, Massachusetts.

The increasing value enjoyed by still-available old figureheads today as nostalgic mementos of the days of sailing ships has unfortunately inspired the counterfeiter as well. Thus, figures newly made and with clever "patinas" made in Scotland have made their way via the antique trade, not only as decorations in hotels, shore restaurants or the houses of private collectors, but also in museums, without their owners necessarily being clear as to their origins. In a major American maritime museum which was given several such forgeries, they have been put away in a storeroom, but in the greatest German collection of figureheads they are on display along with the genuine pieces.

As regrettable as this situation may be, nevertheless it underscores the value placed on figureheads today. And creations of the artist or artisan, whether paintings, furniture, goldsmithing or sculpture, that are profitable to falsify have, of course, always been a yardstick for the general importance of those items. It is to be hoped all the more that the counterfeiters will be followed more and more by artistic research on figureheads and on woodcarving for ships and the artists who created it.

Left: Design drawing for a figurehead for the ship *Queen of Sheba* by John W. Mason, circa 1850; Peabody Museum, Salem, Massachusetts.

Right: Design drawing for a figurehead for the American ship *King Philip* by John W. Mason, circa 1850; Peabody Museum, Salem, Massachusetts.

Bibliography

Ahrens, Hermann & Rittmeister, Wolfgang, *Neptuns hölzerne Engel, Schöne alte Galionsfiguren*, Hamburg 1958.

Asaert, Dr. G., *Westeuropese scheepvaart in de middeleeuwen*, Bussum 1974.

Auguier, Philippe, *Pierre Puget, Decorateur et Mariniste*, Paris, n.d.

Beylen, Jules van, "De versiering van Jachten, Binnenschepen en Visservaartuigen in de Nederlanden," *Neerlands Volksleven*, zomer, Den Haag 1963.

Bjerg, H. C., "Om Soetatens kort—og tegningssamling," *Arkiv 4*, Copenhagen 1973.

Bjerring, K. B., "Stävdekorationerna genom tiderna," *Halland*, Halmstad, 1963.

Booneborg, K., *Scheeps-sier, Ausstellungskatalog Rijksmuseum Zuiderzeemuseum*, Enkhuizen, 1962.

Brewington, M. V., *Shipcarvers of North America*, Barre, MA, 1962.

Bruce-Mitford, R., "Ships' Figureheads in the Migration Period and Early Middle Ages," *Antiquity*, London, 1970.

Carr, Frank G. G., *Maritime Greenwich*, London, 1974.

Carr, Frank G. G., *The Cutty Sark*, London, 1976.

Chapman, Fredrik Henrik af, *Architectura navalis mercatoria*, Stockholm, 1768.

Clark, Arthur H., *The Clipper Ship Era*, New York, 1911.

Dunning, Edgar D., *Landlocked Lady*, Newburyport, MA, 1967.

Ellmers, Detlev, *Frühmittelalterliche Handelsschiffahrt in Mittelund Nordeuropa*, Neumünster, 1972.

Gaunt, William, *Marine Painting*, London, 1975.

Göttlicher, Arvid, *Materialien für ein Corpus der Schiffsmodelle im Altertum*.

Guillen, Julio, "Mascarons," *Archivo Español de Arte y Arqueologia*, Madrid, 1934.

Halldin, Gustaf, "Galjonsbilder och ornament på svenska örlogsskepp," *Samleren*, Stockholm, 1936.

Halldin, Gustaf (ed.), *Svenskt Skeppsbyggeri*, Malmö, 1963.

Hallén, Tore & Rüster, Reijo, *Galjonsbilder*, Stockholm, 1975.

Hansen, Hans Jürgen (ed.), *Kunstgeschichte der Seefahrt*, Oldenburg & Hamburg, 1966.

Hansen, Hans Jürgen, *Schiffsmodelle*, Oldenburg & Hamburg, n.d.

Hansen, Hans Jürgen, *Schiffe, Häfen, Meere und Matrosen*, Oldenburg & Hamburg, 1975.

Hansen, Hans Jürgen, "Galionsfigurenschnitzer auf der Isle of Wight," *Sammlerjournal 11*, Schwäbisch Hall, 1975.

Hansen, Knud E., "Forstaevnsformer," *Handels og Söfartsmuseets Årborg*, Helsingör, 1946.

Hazelhoff Roelfzema, H., "Fotos uit het scheepvaartmuseum 1860-1910," *De Blauwe Wimpel*, Amsterdam, 1970.

Heine, William C., *Historic Ships of the World*, Newton Abbot & London 1977.

Henningsen, Henning, "Galionsfiguren," *Soens Verden*, Copenhagen, 1949-50.

Hornell, James, "Survivals of the Use of Oculi in Modern Boats," *Journal of Royal Anthropological Institute*, London, 1923.

Hornell, James, "Boat Oculi Survivals," *Journal of Royal Anthropological Institute*, London, 1938.

Hornell, James, "The Prow of the Ship," *Journal of Royal Anthropological Institute*, London, 1943.

Höver, Otto, *Von der Galion zum Fünfmaster*, Bremen, 1934.

"Immer mit dem Busen vornweg," *Hamburger Leben*, March, Hamburg, 1975.

Jaeger, Werner, "Eine Nofretete unter den Schiffsmodellen," *Schriften des Deutschen Schiffahrtsmuseums*, Oldenburg & Hamburg, 1978.

Kimball, Fiske, *Mr. Samuel McIntire, Carver*, Portland, ME, 1940.

Köster, August, *Das Antike Seewesen*, Berlin, 1923.

Kraft, Hermann F., *Catalogue of Historic Objects at the United States Naval Academy*, Annapolis, 1925.

Kruissink, G. R., *Scheepssier*, Baarn, 1977.

Laughton, L. G. Carr, *Old Ships Figureheads and Sterns*, London, 1925.

Leander, Ulla, "Galjonsbildhuggaren Johan Törnström 1743-1828," *Blekingeboken*, Karlskrona, 1943.

Lebech, Mogens, *Burmeister & Wain Museum, Katalog*, Copenhagen, 1959.

Marceau, Henri, *Works of William Rush*, Philadelphia, 1937.

Marstal og Omegns Museum, Katalog, Marstal, n.d.

Meyer, Jürgen, "Neuerwerbungen Schiffahrt und Fischerei," *Altonaer Museum in Hamburg, Yearbook*, Vol. 3, Hamburg 1965.

¿page 46¡

Norton, Peter, *Figureheads*, London, 1972.

Norton, Peter, *Ship's Figureheads*, Newton Abbot, London & Vancouver, 1976.

Nyman, Valdemar, "Bland gallionsbilder på Ålands Sjöfartsmuseum," *Sanct Olof*, Vol. 13, Mariehamn, 1977.

Oderwald, J., "Scheepsfolklore in de Scheepsversiering," *Buiten*, Vol. 28, Amsterdam, 1934.

Owen, D., "Figureheads," *Mariners Mirror*, Vol. III, London, 1913.

Pack, A. J. & Dawson, Peter, *The Origins of the Figurehead*, Portsmouth, n.d.

Pardal, Paolo, *Carrancas de Sao Francisco*, Rio de Janeiro, 1974.

Philippovich, Eugen von, "Galionsfiguren," *Kuriositäten, Antiquitäten*, Braunschweig, 1966.

Pinckney, Pauline A., *American Figureheads and Their Carvers*, New York, 1940.

Poulsen, Hanne, *Gallionsfigurer og ornamenter på dankse skibe og i danske samlinger*, Copenhagen, 1976.

Rebuffo, Luciano, *Polene Italiane*, Rome, 1960.

Rehder, Anita, "Galionsfiguren aus dem Museum in Altona," *Die Yacht* 11, Bielefeld, 1978.

Rizzi, Amadeo, *Il Museo delle Navi*, Bologna, n.d.

Rudolph, Wolfgang, *Boote, Flösse, Schiffe*, Leipzig, 1974.

Schäuffelen, Otmar, *Die letzten grossen Segelschiffe*, Bielefeld & Berlin, 1973.

Schlechtriem, Gert., "Galionsfigurenschnitzer im Deutschen Schiffahrtsmuseum," *Kunst und Museen in Bremen und Bremerhaven*, Bremen, 1977.

Severance, Frank, *Historic Figureheads*, Buffalo, 1921.

Stackpole, Edward A., *Figureheads and Ship Carvings at Mystic Seaport*, Mystic, CT, 1964.

Soop, Hans, *Regalskeppet Wasa, Skulpturer*, Stockholm, 1978. "The Art of the Shipcarver at the Peabody Museum of Salem," *The American Neptune*, Salem, MA, 1977.

Timmermann, Gerhard, "Galionsfiguren," *Ausstellungskatalog Altonaer Museum*, Hamburg, 1961.

Wietek, Gerhard, "Galionsfiguren im Altonaer Museum," *Die Kunst und das schöne Heim*, Munich, 1978.

Illustrations

THE PHOTOGRAPHS OF THE ILLUSTRATED OBJECTS WERE FOR THE MOST PART KINDLY MADE AVAILABLE BY THEIR POSSESSORS. IN ADDITION, PHOTOGRAPHIC MATERIAL, PARTICULARLY IN COLOR, WAS PROVIDED BY HANS GULDBRANDSEN, CLAS BRODER HANSEN, WALTER LUDEN, EVELINDE MANON, GUNTER MEIERDIERKS, JAN WASSERMANN AND BENNO WUNDSHAMMER.

Page 49: Figure of a lion, 18th Century, 238 cm; Statens Sjöhistoriska Museum, Stockholm (S).

Upper left: Half-figure of a man from the Norwegian ship *Viktor*, grounded near Hulberga, Brändö, in 1870, 92 cm; Sjöhistoriska Museet vid Åbo Akademi, Turku (SF).

Upper right: Feminine bust with green blouse, latter half of 19th Century, 40 cm; Cutty Sark Society, Greenwich, London (GB).

Page 51: Half-figure of a sailor in the style of the late Victorian *Jack Tar*, from the 12-gun British brig *Daring*, built 1844 at Portsmouth, wrecked 1864; National Maritime Museum, Greenwich, London (GB).

Page 52: Feminine figure from the ship *Maren*, 130 cm; Heimatmuseum, Schönebeck, Bremen (D).

Page 53: Masculine half-figure in Scottish dress, circa 1830, 117 cm; Deutsches Schiffahrtmuseum, Bremerhaven (D).

Upper left: Masculine bust with blue cap, red jacket and gold epaulettes, from the ship *Forfarshire*, 55 cm; Barrack Street Museum, Dundee (GB).

Upper right: Masculine bust, first half of the 19th Century, from the whaler *Commodore Morris*, built 1841, 90 cm; The Mariners Museum, Newport News, VA (USA).

Page 55: Three-quarter figure of a boy with a sailor hat, 85 cm; Bornholms Museum, Ronne (DK).

Page 56: Full figure of the muse Thalia, probably from the shipyard of Ernst Dreyer, Neuhof am Reiherstieg, first half of the 19th Century, ca. 170 cm; Altonaer Museum, Hamburg (D).

Page 57: Half-figure of the Bavarian Queen Caroline from the pleasure ship *Caroline* of King Maximilian I, early 19th Century, 76 cm; Heimatmuseum, Starnberg (D).

Upper left: Half-figure of Admiral de Ruyter with insignia of an order, 111 cm; Rijksmuseum, Amsterdam (NL).

Upper right: Masculine half-figure from the freighter *Cambria*, built 1846 in London, 170 cm; Museo Navale, La Spezia (I).

Page 59: Figure of Neptune riding a dolphin between two winged tritons, from Napoleon's state boat, built 1811 in Antwerp, carved by Van Petersen, gilded, life-size; Musée de la Marine, Paris (F).

59

Page 60: Three-quarter figure of a woman, probably first half of the 19th Century, 80 cm; Friesenmuseum, Wyk auf Föhr (D).

Page 61: Feminine three-quarter figure of the goddess Diana from a British ship, latter half of the 19th Century; Wrackmuseum, Cuxhaven (D).

Upper left: Woman's head, remains of a figure symbolizing the Weser River, from the ocean liner *Weser II*, built 1867 in Greenock, Scotland, 45 cm; Focke-Museum, Bremen (D).

Upper right: Feminine head, probably of the goddess Minerva, from the ship *Minerva* of Tonsberg, 84 cm, Norsk Sjofartsmuseum, Oslo (N).

Page 63: Feminine half-figure with red blouse, 19th Century, 183 cm; Cutty Sark Society, Greenwich, London (GB).

Page 64: Double figure of mother and child, circa 1840-50, 80 cm; Handelsog Sofartsmuseet på Kronborg, Helsingor (DK).

Upper left: Feminine three-quarter figure, mid-19th Century, 85 cm; Norsk Sjofartsmuseum, Oslo (N).

Upper right: Feminine figure found at Sable Island, 142 cm; Nova Scotia Museum, Halifax, Nova Scotia (CDN).

Page 66: Half-figure of a sailor, circa 1840-50, 80 cm; Handels- og Søfartsmuseet på Kronborg, Helsingør (DK).

Page 67: Half-figure of a man from the full-rigged school ship *Danmark*, built 1933 in Nakskov, 105 cm; Heimathafen, Copenhagen (DK).

Upper left: Half-figure of Christopher Columbus from the Sardinian brigantine *Cristoforo Colombo*, built 1843 in Genoa, 142 cm; Museo Navale, La Spezia (I).

Upper right: Masculine bust, probably portraying Admiral Duquesne, from the ship *Duquesne*, built 1853 in Brest, 171 cm; Musée de la Marine, Paris (F).

Page 69: Feminine bust in antique dress, from the frigate *La Couronne*, built 1861 in Lorient, 126 cm; Musée de la Marine, Paris (F).

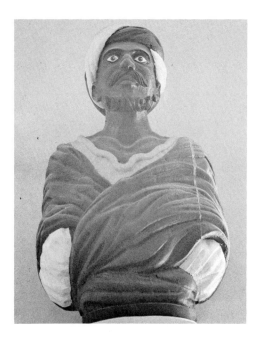

Page 70: Three-quarter figure of Niels Jul, from the Danish frigate *Niels Juel*, built 1855 at the royal shipyard in Copenhagen, flagship of the Danish North Sea Squadron in the battle of Helgoland, May 9, 1864; carved from a design by Julius Magnus Petersen, more than life-size, Fladeståtion,, Holmen, Copenhagen (DK).

Page 71: Figure of a siren, from the state boat *La Marie-Thérèse* of Queen Marie Antoinette, built 1777 at Versailles, 171 cm; Musée de la Marine, Paris (F).

Upper left: Masculine half-figure from the bark *Hindu*, built 1850, 90 cm; Heimatmuseum, Schönebeck Castle, Bremen (D).

Upper right: Figure of a Roman warrior, from the ship *City of Rome*, built 1871 in Liverpool, 200 cm; Heimatmuseum, Schönebeck, Bremen (D).

Page 73: Feminine quarter-figure, ca. 120 cm; Altonaer Museum, Hamburg (D).

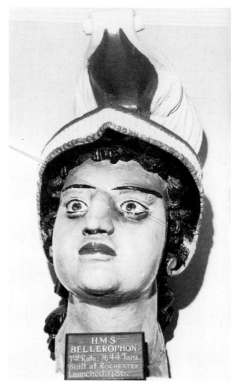

Page 74: Three-quarter figure of a Scottish grenadier, from the ship *Grenadier*, built 1885 by J. & G. Thomson, 150 cm; Glasgow Museum & Gallery, Glasgow (GB).

Page 75: Feminine three-quarter figure, from the ship *Helen Denny*, built 1866 by Duncan, Port Glasgow, 150 cm; Glasgow Museum & Gallery, Glasgow (GB).

Upper left: Head of a warrior, from the British warship *Warrior*, built 1871 in Portsmouth, wrecked 1857; Victory Museum, Portsmouth (GB).

Upper right: Feminine head, from the British warship *Bellerophon*, built 1786 in Rochester; Victory Museum, Portsmouth (GB).

Page 77: Masculine three-quarter figure, from the Brigantine *Bosphorus*; Valhalla Maritime Museum, Tresco, Scilly Isles (GB).

Page 78: Feminine half-figure, 19th Century, 76 cm;
Cutty Sark Society, Greenwich, London (GB).

Page 79: Feminine quarter-figure, probably from the
British ship *Georgina*, 19th Century, 91 cm; Cutty
Sark Society, Greenwich, London (GB).

Upper left: Half-figure of a chieftainess with feathers,
from the ship *Awashonks*, built 1830 at Woods Hole,
Falmouth, MA, 100 cm; Whaling Museum, New
Bedford, MA (USA).

Upper right: Masculine bust in Oriental dress, from
the British warship *Carnatic*, built 1823 in
Portsmouth; Victory Museum, Portsmouth (GB).

Page 81: Feminine three-quarter figure from a French
merchant ship of the 18th Century; National
Maritime Museum, Greenwich, London (GB).

Page 82: Masculine half-figure, from the British warship *Rodney*, built 1884, 221 cm; Royal Naval Dockyard, Chatham (GB).

Upper left: Masculine bust from an Austrian warship, first half of the 19th Century, 110 cm; Heeresgeschichtliches Museum, Wien (A).

Upper right: Feminine full figure, from the schooner *Saida* of the Austro-Hungarian Navy, built 1852-1855 in Venice, 195 cm; Heeresgeschichtliches Museum, Wien (A).

Upper left: Bust of the Greek general Leonidas, King of Sparta, with orange helmet, black feather and blue tunic, from the ship *Leonidas*, built 1826 at the Chittenden Shipyard, Scituate, MA. 81 cm; Whaling Museum, New Bedford, MA (USA).

Upper right: Masculine half-figure, 193 cm, Mystic Seaport, Mystic, CT (USA).

Page 85: Bust of a negress, probably from the ship *Queen of Sheba*, built 1850 in Newcastle or 1853 in Blyth (GB), 47 cm; The Mariners Museum, Newport News, VA (USA).

85

Above, left to right: Feminine half-figure in a blue dress, from the schooner *Jane Owen* of Caernarvon, built 1860 in Pwlheli, wrecked 1889 on Queens Ledge; feminine half-figure in red bodice and blue cloak; male half-figure with high collar, dark coat and red vest, from the ship *Roseville*, wrecked 1855; male figure in uniform with gun, from coaster *Volunteer*, Valhalla Museum, Tresco, Scilly Isles (GB).

Page 87 left: Feminine full figure by a French-Canadian carver, probably John Rogerson, 195 cm; Museet for Haugesund og Bygdene, Haugesund (N).

Page 87 right: Feminine full figure in Roman tunic and armor, probably starboard figure from the Sardinian frigate *Italia*, former Neapolitan ship *Farnese*, built 1861 by Maudslay in London, 189 cm; Museo Navale, La Spezia (I).

Page 88: Full masculine figure from the ship *Polinarus*, sunk 1848; Valhalla Maritime Museum, Tresco, Scilly Isles (GB).

Upper Left: Feminine half-figure in Biedermeier clothing and hair style, circa 1835, 93 cm; New York State Historical Association, Cooperstown, NY (USA).

Upper right: Half-figure of Lord Aberdeen, from the merchant ship *Varo*, former British *Lord Aberdeen*, in Sardinian naval service since 1855, 91 cm; Musel Navale, La Spezia (I).

Upper left: Feminine half-figure, from the British warship *Bulwark*, built 1859; HMS *Pembroke*, Chatham (GB).

Upper right: Full figure of the victory goddess Victoria, from funeral barge that carried Lord Nelson from Greenwich to his burial in St. Paul's Cathedral, London, built 1805, ca. 90 cm; National Maritime Museum, Greenwich, London (GB).

Page 91: Feminine three-quarter figure with yellow blouse and green skirt, latter half of the 19th Century, 76 cm; Cutty Sark Society, Greenwich, London (GB).

Page 92: Male half-figure, 152 cm; Ringkjobing Museum, Ringkobing (DK)

Upper left: Half-figure of Queen Victoria from the Sicilian warship *Baleno,* ex *Fairy Queen,* built 1860 in London, 215 cm; Museo Navale, La Spezia (I).

Upper right: Half-figure of Empress Elisabeth, from the Austrian paddle steamer *Elisabeth Kaiserin,* built 1889. 150 cm; Museo Navale, La Spezia (I).

Upper left: Half-figure of a harlequin, from the British sloop *Harlequin*, built 1836 at Pembroke, wrecked 1889, 152 cm; National Maritime Museum, Greenwich, London (GB).

Upper right: Full figure of a kneeling girl, from a 19th-Century Portuguese ship, ca. 100 cm; Christian Ahrenkiel, Nieblum on Föhr (D).

Page 95: Feminine quarter-figure, from the ship *Freedom*, U.S. Naval Academy Museum, Annapolis, MD (USA).

 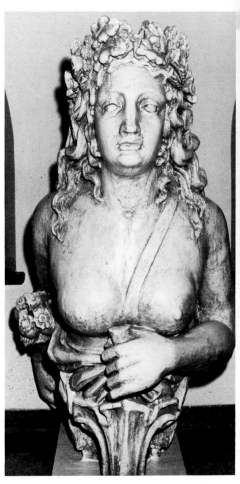

Upper left: Feminine half-figure with crown, symbol of the City of London, from the British warship *London*, built 1840 at Chatham, converted to steam 1858, wrecked 1884, 275 cm; National Maritime Museum, Greenwich, London (GB).

Upper right: Feminine quarter-figure, from the Prussian frigate *Hertha*, built 1860-65 at the Royal Shipyard, Danzig; Deutsches Schiffahrtsmuseum, Bremerhaven (D).

Page 97: Full feminine figure, latter half of the 19th Century, 112 cm; Cutty Sark Society, Greenwich, London (GB).

Page 98: Male half-figure, from the ship *Willem de Zwyger*, 97 cm; Bredasdorp Museum, Bredasdorp (ZA).

Upper left: Full sitting figure of a young man, Musée de St. Malo, St. Malo (F).

Upper right: Figure of the American hero David Crockett, from the clipper *David Crockett*, built 1853 by Greenman & Co., Mystic, CT, carved by Jacob Andersen, 244 cm; San Francisco Maritime Museum, San Francisco CA (USA).

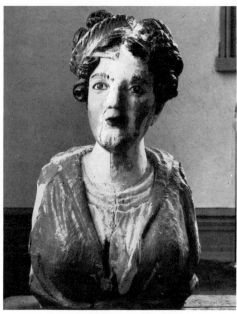

Page 100: Figureheads from the Cutty Sark Collection in Greenwich before restoration; the figure at upper right has been restored.

Page 101: Full male figure, 19th Century; National Maritime Museum, Greenwich, London (GB).

Upper left: Feminine quarter-figure, from the Norwegian bark *Salween*, wrecked 1895, ca. 65 cm; Volunteer Life Brigade, South Shields (GB).

Upper right: Feminine quarter-figure, 72 cm; Ringkjobing Museum, Ringkobing (DK)

Page 103: Feminine head, 19th Century; Ringkjobing Museum, Ringkóbing (DK)

Page 104: Three-quarter figure of a Saracen warrior, probably from the British warship *Himalaya*, a bark-rigged iron screw steamer, built 1851 by C. J. Mare in Blackwall, transport in Crimean War, coal hulk "C 60" at Devonport until about 1896, sold 1920, sunk 1940 in an air raid at Portland; National Maritime Museum, Greenwich, London (GB).

Page 105: Head of Lord Nelson, his right (blind) eye closed, on a scroll, from the 46-gun British warship *Horatio*, built 1807 by George Parson at Burlesdon, Hampshire; National Maritime Museum, Greenwich, London (GB).

Upper left: Feminine figure, from Prussian warship *Vineta*, built 1860-64 at the royal Shipyard, Danzig; Historical Collection of the Mürwik Naval School, Flensburg (D).

Upper right: Full feminine figure, from German warship *Deutschland*, built 1904 at Kiel, wrecked 1922, ca. 250 cm; Underwater Weapons School of the Federal Navy; Eckernförde (D).

Page 107: Full feminine figure of Maria Parés, daughter of D. Silvestre Parés, owner and captain of the *Blanca Aurora*, 1862, in regional dress, from ship *Tres Hermanas*, ex *Bianca Aurora*, built 1848 as *Ferreret* by Agustin Pujol in Lloret de Mar, Greona, wrecked 1883, carved 1848 by Francisco Pascual y Granés, called *Ulls Menuts*, 125 cm; Museo Maritimo, Barcelona (E).

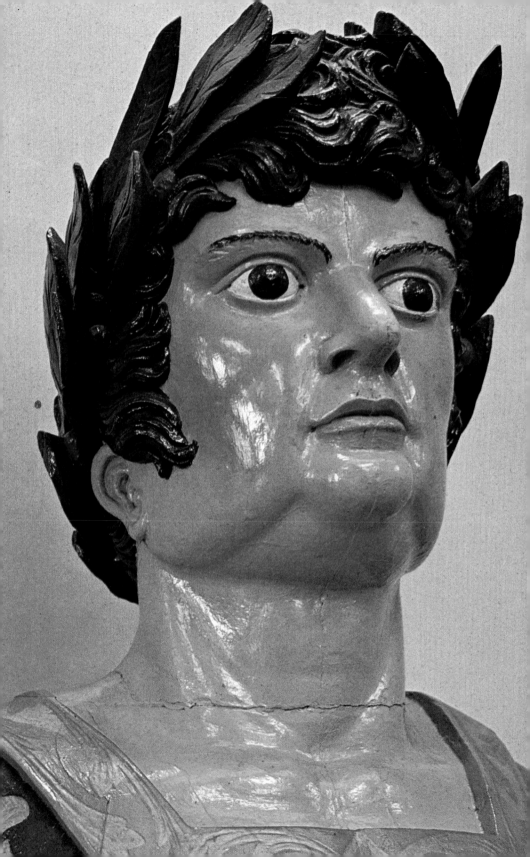

Page 108: Bust of King George IV as Roman emperor, from 120-gun British warship *Royal George*, ex *Neptune*, built 1827 at Chatham, 152 cm; National Maritime Museum, Greenwich, London (GB).

Page 109: Half-figure of a river god, from British warship *Dee* (brigantine-rigged wooden steamer), built 1832 at Woolwich, wrecked 1871, 140 cm; National Maritime Museum, Greenwich, London (GB).

Upper left: Portrait bust of King Fredrik V, flanked by male and female figures, wax model of figurehead for the Danish warship *Fridericus Quintus*, built 1753 at the Royal Shipyard, Copenhagen, 32 cm; Orlogsmuseet, Copenhagen (DK).

Upper right: Masculine figure fighting lions; wax model of figurehead for the Danish warship *Oldenborg*, built 1740 at Royal Shipyard, Copenhagen, 33 cm; Orlogsmuseet, Copenhagen (DK).

Page 111, left to right: Figure of victory goddess Victoria from warship *Karl XIII*, built 1819, carved by Johan Törnström ca. 1820, 400 cm; full antique feminine figure with shield bearing the arms of Göteborg, from the frigate *Göteborg*, ex *Minerva*, carved by Johan Tornström in 1784, 360 cm; full figure of King Carl XIV Johan (Charles Baptiste Bernadotte) in Roman dress, from warship *Carl XIV Johan*, built 1824, carved by Emanuel Törnström, 320 cm; Marinmuseum, Karlskrona (S).

Page 112: Full feminine figure, probably from a Spanish ship; Valhalla Maritime Museum, Tresco, Scilly Isles (GB).

Upper left: Feminine bust on scroll with shields and leaves, portraying Prussian Crown Princess Cecilie, from the four-masted bark *Herzogin Cecilie*, built 1902 by Rickmers, Bremerhaven, wrecked 1936 on the Devon coast while underway from Falmouth to Ipswich, carved 1902, 300 cm; Ålands Sjöfartsmuseum, Marienhamn, Åland (SF).

Upper right: Feminine three-quarter figure, from the iron bark *Loch Linnhe*, built 1876 by J. & G. Thomson, Glasgow, for a German firm, sold 1922 to Erikson line, Marienhamn, wrecked 1933 on Flisskäret, Riff of Kökar, 280 cm; Ålands Sköfartsmuseum, Marienhamn, Åland (SF).

Page 114: Three-quarter figure of a negro, from the ship *Wylo*, built 1869 by Robert Steele in Greenock, 115 cm; Fries Scheepvaart Museum, Sneek (NL).

Page 115: Full feminine figure from Norwegian school ship *Christian Radich* (still afloat), built 1937 by Framnaes Mekaniske Verkstadt, Sandefjord, ca. 200 cm; Heimathafen Oslo (N).

Upper left: Feminine three-quarter figure missing its arms, perhaps from mail ship *Jenny Lind*, built 1848, or clipper *Nightingale*, built 1851, 99 cm; The Mariners Museum, Newport News, VA (USA).

Upper right: Figurehead of schooner *Ploughboy*, wrecked 1891, ca. 60 cm; Volunteer Life Brigade, South Shields (GB).

Page 117: Figurehead of schooner *Mail*, wrecked 1862, ca. 64 cm, Volunteer Life Brigade, South Shields (GB).

Page 118: Feminine three-quarter figure, from ship *Charlotte*, 90 cm; Rauman Museo, Rauma (SF).

Page 119: Feminine figure, probably from a galleot wrecked on the Jutland coast in 1820, 60 cm; Schiffahrtsmuseum, Brake (D).

Upper left: Half-figure of a naval officer, 19th Century, 200 cm; Altonaer Museum, Hamburg (D).

Upper right: Half-figure of a naval officer, 19th Century, 193 cm; Altonaer Museum, Hamburg (D).

Page 121: Male half-figure, probably of a naval officer, circa 1800; Valhalla Maritime Museum, Tresco, Scilly Isles (GB).

Page 122: Full feminine figure, either from the ship *Osage* or *Rose in Bloom*, both built ca. 1810-14 at Essex, CT, 93 cm; The Mariners Museum, Newport News, VA (USA).

Page 123: Male half-figure of a Turk or Indian, ca. 145 cm; Mystic Seaport, Mystic, CT (USA).

Upper left: Lion figure, from 74-gun British warship *Hogue*, built 1808-11 at Deptford, wrecked 1869, one of the last examples of lion figureheads, common on British warships since the times of Queen Elizabeth I (1558-1603); National Maritime Museum, Greenwich, London (GB).

Upper right: Full lion figure from a ship wrecked on the west coast of Jutland, mid-17th Century, 200 cm; Handelsog Sofartsmuseet på Kronborg, Helsingor (DK).

Above: Dog's head, probably from Swedish privateer
Vinthunden, ca. 1711, whose captain was the pirate
Lars Gathenhielm, captured by the Danes in 1716,
though the acanthus leaves suggest an origin toward
the end of the 18th Century, 100 cm; Sjöfartsmuseet,
Göteborg (S).

Page 126: Figure of actor François Joseph Talma
playing Roman Emperor Nero, probably from ship
Talma, built 1827 at Medford, MA, probably carved
Isaac Fowle, 213 cm; Peabody Museum, Salem, MA
(USA).

Page 127: Figure of a Scotsman from a 19th-Century
ship, 160 cm; Peabody Museum, Salem, MA (USA).

Contents